FLUFFYBUTT LOVE

Healing with Wings

Jessie Shedden

JessieShedden.Com

Copyright © 2021 Jessie Shedden

Fluffybutt Love
Written by Jessie Shedden
Copyright © Jessie Shedden
No part of this book may be reproduced, stored in a retrieval system, transmitted in any form or by any means, electronic, mechanical, photocopying, recording or otherwise without the prior permission of the authors; the only exception being quotes and/or excerpts for review.

Publisher's Note: All stories and quotes appear with the permission and courtesy of individual contributors.

Fluffybutt Love
www.jessieshedden.com/fluffybuttlove https://www.facebook.com/fluffybuttloves https://www.facebook.com/groups/loveoffluffybutts

All rights reserved.

*Dedicated to all my wonderful girls who have crossed over rainbow bridge already:
Lena, Amber, Cottia, Lady, Fluffball, Creamy, Natter, Chamois. And to those still loving us daily: Cuddlepot, Chamois Deux, Pretty, Blue, Noire, and Butterscotch.
– You Loved First.*

Jessie Shedden

CONTENTS

Title Page	1
Copyright	2
Dedication	3
Preface	9
Foreword	12
Introduction	16
Chapter 1	30
Chapter 2	34
Chapter 3	41
Chapter 4	45
Chapter 5	49
Chapter 6	54
Chapter 7	70
Chapter 8	72
Chapter 9	76
Chapter 10	86
Chapter 11	89
Chapter 12	93
Chapter 13	95

Chapter 14	99
Chapter 15	101
Chapter 16	108
Chapter 17	110
Chapter 18	112
Chapter 19	113
Chapter 20	116
Chapter 21	119
Chapter 22	121
Chapter 23	123
Chapter 24	125
Chapter 25	127
Chapter 26	131
Chapter 27	133
Chapter 28	136
Chapter 29	139
Chapter 30	141
Chapter 31	144
Chapter 32	147
Chapter 33	150
Chapter 34	152
Chapter 35	154
Chapter 36	157
Chapter 37	159
Chapter 38	162
Chapter 39	165

Chapter 40	167
Chapter 41	171
Chapter 42	172
Chapter 43	176
Chapter 44	178
Meet the Contributors	180
Share With Us	194
Who is Jessie Shedden?	195
More Fluffybutt Love?	197
More in the book series	199
Glossary	200

Acknowledgements:

Joe Nutkins, Wolfie, Mel Lazenby, Eden Zook, Margaret Hope, Sarah Seleta Nothnagel, Aspen Palmer, Nicky Dawson, Lizzie Harling, Wendy Steele, Dawna June, Dean Burton, E.V. Dawson, Wendy Rurak, Marion Petersen, Virginia Hill, Connie Sides, Linda Eblett, Bonney A.R., Stephanie F Kelley, Amanda Quire, Rebecca Robinson, Clare Kinkley, Emily Rose Thorpe, Jolene Kunde, James Weatherup, Emma Mitchell, Libby Downes, Marissa Troxclair, Natalie Mcteer, Sue Ball, Shirley Acreman, Mandy Watts, Clare Hawkesby, Judith Fletcher King, Sarah Banner, K.L. Smith, Tiggy Fuller, Bess Elle, Lena Zaiceva.

PREFACE

Picture the scene...

It's 2020 and the world is locked in and locked down and turning to both their pets and the internet for love, connection and support. But the very reason we desire all of these wonderful feelings is because we are hurting and frustrated....

.... And then in this tinderbox environment, someone lights a match in one of the 21 different Facebook chicken groups I peruse, and 352,840 people hover their fingers over their screens deciding if they will succumb to cabin fever and vent, pouring out all of their pain and exasperation. And just like that, the love that we all have for chickens' morphs into a maelstrom of emotions that are anything but love.

Many abandon groups struggling to filter love from keyboard fights, others leave Facebook entirely. But the chicken love remains and that, my friend, is where Fluffybutt Love comes in.

A heart-warming book series of inspirational true stories of the feathered fowl we love so well. Think Jack Canfields 'Chicken Soup for the Soul' – only with a lot less soup and a lot *more* chickens.

Did you know that blind chickens could learn the difference between different verbal instructions? Nope, neither did I!

Or that somewhere on a mountain in North Wales chickens were responsible for the healing of their tutu-wearing Harley-riding owner after she woke up from a 5-week coma pretty much paralyzed from the neck down?

Or indeed that your favourite rooster may in fact not be unwell, but actually completely rat-arsed?!

Or that in homes all across the world, there are very special little feathery fowl who have wheedled their way inside their owner's homes and a number of those love nothing better than to watch the TV and doze beside said owners at night? No, neither did I! (Trying to figure how to break that one to my partner right now!)

Within these pages, you will read about all of that and much more including plenty of examples of that long-held phenomenon we all know as *Chicken Math*.

In our Online Facebook Fluffybutt Community (facebook.com/groups/loveoffluffybutts, you can find the owners of the fowls featured within these pages, ever ready to talk at length about their dearly loved feathered friends.

FOREWORD

What began as a day of pottering at home lead to an invitation to write the foreword for the first book of the Fluffybutt Love series. A very unlikely and incredibly honouring request to receive on an otherwise dull weekday afternoon.

As a mental health nurse, having worked throughout the COVID19 pandemic and who specializes in safeguarding and having an active caseload of domestic violence, child protection and sexual exploitation cases, it's been a stressful few months and I've needed my down time more than ever before.

I'm also a hen rescuer and have been involved with Fresh Start for Hens, a not-for-profit voluntary group who rescue and rehome ex-commercial hens from the egg production sector, for around a decade. I'm one of the most senior volunteers within the organization, a bit of a dog's-body- the go-to girl and pretty good chicken whisperer to boot!

When I was asked to write this, my first thought was

'Who is Jessie and what's she all about?' so I did a bit of research and realized how much her own story, told in her previous book, *Tomorrow's Not Promised,* reflects some of the experiences of many of the clients I work with and how very similar our journeys into hen keeping have been on an emotional level.

There's no better therapy at the end of a stressful day than that provided by a hen sitting in your lap and purring, and to me, the feeling's even more special when that hen's a rescued one who's been given a second chance. *Who needs a staff debrief when they have chicken cuddles waiting at home?*

Fresh Start for Hens began as a small group in the south of England and has grown immensely in the last decade or so, with increasing public demand for better welfare standards and awareness of the plight of the commercial egg-laying hen. Social media has given us a wide-reaching voice and a platform to spread the word as far and wide as we can. And boy, have we done that!

Last year alone, during the COVID-19 pandemic and the limitations placed on us, we still managed to save and rehome 67,025 hens from egg farms just before their "expiry date" at just 72 weeks old. That's a huge number and living proof that the word's getting out there.

My own hen keeping journey and how I found myself in my current role with Fresh Start for Hens was inevitable. I knew I wanted to keep a few backyard hens and it had to be rescue girls.... that's just who I am and how I do things!

I persuaded my then partner that it was a good idea; we built a coop and run, got in touch with Fresh Start for Hens, adopted five hens a few weeks later and I became an active part of the online hen keeping community. At the time, I lived in an urban setting and couldn't upsize my flock, but the love story had begun! I took to them like the proverbial "duck to water" and the path was laid out ahead of me.

From there on, I've hosted collection days regularly for the last 8-9 years, seeing literally thousands upon thousands of hens placed into safe retirement homes. I've become a senior member of the volunteer team and am a moderator on our social media groups as well as a member of the very busy reservations team. I quickly discovered an affinity with the "poorly" hens and have become one of the organizations go-to girls when helps needed with caring for any who are sick or injured. I guess my background training as a nurse might have come into play here, but I'm a natural with the neediest of them!

A hen is a hen no matter her breed and background; whether she's a rescue hen, a Bluebelle, a Frizzle or a Serama, a Leghorn, a Bantam or a Brahma, each has a unique personality, and each is able to wrap herself around our hearts. The more opportunities we have to introduce them as pets, as companion animals and as family members the better. And what better way to do that than by publishing the real-life stories of some of them and the humans they've captivated? The humour, the love, the worries, the healing, the muck and the magic they bring. The reality of sharing our lives with them, sometimes warts and all.

My partner and I currently have a flock of 10 ex-commercial hens of our own, all of whom arrived here in the "unfit for rehoming" category and have been nursed back to health, albeit many of them have permanent disabilities or special needs. We also have a glorious one-eyed rescue cockerel, Caesar, who's story is featured in this book. It was his story that led to mine and Jessie's introduction and to me being asked to write this piece.

Perhaps his and some of the other stories will warm hearts and inspire a few more people to follow our paths into the world of fluffy butt love! Be warned though, it tends to be a one-way path of no return!

Emma Mitchell – Fresh Start for Hens (FSFH)

INTRODUCTION

Unlike almost everyone I know, I spent the first 30 years of my life growing up in a strict religious cult, one in which pets were strictly forbidden. That's right dogs, cats, goldfish and hamsters were banned. * See footnote on page 26

Chickens, however, were allowed, on the premise that they laid eggs, so they were useful. However, that was the only basis. You were definitely not expected to love them, and as soon as they started 'freeloading' you were expected to get rid of them.

These beautiful beings were not something you were to respect or develop an emotional connection with. So, in true Jessie fashion – I, of course, did!

Because, as an undiscovered dyslexic, being home-schooled was frankly depressing and with all my siblings being eight-plus years older than me, it left me feeling devoid of any human company, so when my mother suggested getting 5 chickens my world turned on its axis.

Flinging open the back door after my studies were finished for the day and plonking myself down on the concrete block that acted as a back step, as my flock half ran, half flew into my lap for cuddles was without a doubt the highlight of my day.

But little did I know what lay ahead. Thanks to the regulations of the cult, we were sent community families to entertain each week for Sunday lunch. Families whose children had not been instructed in how to treat animals with love and respect and while their mothers sipped Port and fathers knocked back a Whisky or two, the children wanted to run off all their unspent energy in the garden after sitting still for 2 hours in the church service from which they'd just come.

And what better way than to terrorize and torment creatures which you did not appreciate and had no concept of understanding.

Each week as Sunday's rolled around, I would feel sick in the pit of my stomach as I scanned the list of names assigned to devour my mother's delicious Sunday Roast and determine how many children I'd need to protect my beloved flock from today.

As always when you stand up to bullies, you run the risk of not only directing attention to yourself as a target but also of actually increasing the bullying of the subjects you are trying to protect. And these occasions were no exception.

My parents garden was home to my birds and a place they deserved to feel safe in, not being able to provide them with this crippled me with pain.

Unsurprisingly there came a time when my flock aged and as their egg-laying days were over, I was informed that it was time to donate them to a nearby petting zoo. I was lucky in that it was within walking distance so if I was feeling exceptionally low, I'd sneak off out and visit them – only to find that one by one they would disappear due to them not being shut in at night.

The time came and went, and I found myself entering the world of work, but still, the chicken shaped void gaped wide open. So, when our family unit moved to a house that came with a garden 4 times the size of our last one, I knew it was time to get buying chickens again.

With unconditional love in short supply in my surroundings I opted to buy day-old chicks again like I had the first time I needed the fluffy love in my life: and I wanted closeness and for these wee creatures to learn they could trust me.

Seven. That was the number.

Not knowing better, I kept them in the 'Boot Room' which is practically a conservatory and receives masses of sun. We leave for church one Saturday morning and when I return home, I discover that not only had the sun been beaming in on them for the last two hours in addition to their heat bulb, but not a single window is open, the place is akin to a furnace and they have knocked their water over.

Several are already on their backs with their legs in the air barely clinging on to life. I break open the back door, drag the entire box outside into the cool air and rush to give them water. I fight to bring them back, one of my Welsummers doesn't make it. My gorgeous little Pengu lookalike, Lady, my lavender Araucana doesn't look at all promising.

My family continue as though nothing much has happened, my father knows that later he'll have me plead with him to dig a shallow grave in the garden for my Welsummer. Not yet fully understanding my capacity to love beings so little respected by those around me, I tell him we'll not bury her yet as Lady is likely to join her by the end of the day, and I leave Lady to sadly pass away.

Only she doesn't. By evening she's still hanging on and as no help is being offered by anyone else around me, including my mother who is the family doctor and knows all things, I scour the small amount of internet that I am permitted to have access to, on how I may be able to best care for this fluff ball who so needs my care.

Force feed her water it says. It was nightfall now so I set her in a little box on my bedroom dresser and set my alarm to go off at 15-minute intervals throughout the night, so I could pad over to her hunched-up frame and drip her vital supply line off a teaspoon.

We had to leave for church communion at 6 AM and I feared what I'd find when I returned, but Lady wasn't going anywhere. My little bundle of fluff was a tough little girl and through our experience, we bonded stronger than ever.

The weeks ticked past and soon it became apparent there were two rather handsome roosters in my flock! Well, this wasn't on, they didn't lay eggs so unless I was going to breed with them, I would not be permitted to keep them.

I didn't have time to decide if I was going to breed with them as our ever-complaining dictatorial neighbour leaned over the fence one day and informed my father that if he didn't sort them out, he would finish them off himself. In turn, I was promptly told that I would need to 'walk' them – in other words, dump them in a field somewhere, as was considered standard practice.

The very next week just after communion, I was made to collect up my gorgeous Lord Aru, my lavender Araucana and with my mother, at the wheel, we drove out to a village nearby. To this day I can still see the puzzlement in his look as he watched me walk away and leave him there and feel my chest tighten with pain.

Lord Goldlace was a gorgeous Poland boy and, as a bantam, his crow was quieter, as I played for time. I experimented with an anti-crow collar, but he was having none of it! He tried everything from doing a fabulous job of feigning dead to marching backwards around the garden and off a low wall in an effort to get away from this bulky Velcro contraption, to ripping it off over and over again with his little claws!

If only he knew that I was trying my darndest to keep him in the flock. It was not to be, so when the ever-increasing pressure for him to be 'walked' could no longer be ignored I retorted, 'If you want him gone, you'll have to do it because I'm not.' After my experience with Lord Aru, nothing was going to make me do that again.

So once again after our 6 AM communion on Sunday my mother disappeared off in the car and that was the last myself and Lord Goldlace's wife Chamois ever saw of him. Just a month later Chamois broke down, her fabulous counterpart had always protected her from the bullying of my two big Welsummers and without him by her side she no longer wanted to go on.

Birds were cheap and spending out on their care or consulting a vet was not a consideration as far as my mother was concerned, and bringing birds into the house was out of the question too. I'd failed yet another bird and a part of me died when Chamois passed away in such pitiful circumstances in that dark cold boot room before she'd even laid a single egg. I'm not sure we even deserved them.

A year passed and Cuddlepot, one of my two bantams Barbu d'Uccle Millie Fleur's, went broody. I'd never had a broody hen before and given how adorable she was I knew that she'd make a fabulous mother, and her sweet, sweet temperament had won over the hearts of my family more than any bird ever had. So that was that. A quick trawl of eBay and I'd procured some Poland eggs for her after I'd lost both of the Poland's I'd hand-reared before.

I busied myself setting up her nursery and she, like the dependable ball of fluff that I knew her for, did the rest. If you've never seen Cuddlepot's breed before you'll underestimate just how tiny they are – I'm only a short gal but she fitted snuggly in the palm of my hand, so six Poland eggs under her fitted just right!

My love tank overflowed when she proceeded to hatch me a gorgeous Buff Lace and a kind of white* Frizzle! I'd never had a Frizzle before and truth be known I hadn't wanted one, I thought they looked messy.

So, like the parent whose worst fears are realized when their child is born with some disfigurement, I felt only profound guilt for ever having wished for *'anything but a Frizzle'* and found myself falling fast for her gorgeous silky soft plumage. Chamois Deux and Pretty had entered my world.

Sadly, though in just a few weeks I would have to leave them in the care of my siblings while I spent 3 weeks in Mexico with my parents as my mother sought treatment for her advanced cancer.

Oh, how I missed being there for those early days and the comfort and love they brought to the sadness of that period. They couldn't possibly know that life was about to change massively for them, because their human mom was just about to take the biggest leap of her life. She was doing the unthinkable and escaping the cult she'd grown up in.

Unable to take my entire flock of nine with me to my new much smaller rented property, I opted to rehome 5 of them with the daughter of a friend and place the remaining four in temporary care while I moved.

I couldn't wait to collect them and have their company to fill the emptiness of my new property – slowly learning over time to respect and allow my love for them to freely flow, no longer being put down by those around me for being my authentic self – a crazy chicken lady. Being winter they soon found their way into my kitchen and took up residence on my heated floor.

The joy was sadly marred by the sudden and tragic passing of my beloved Lady Aru. In all that I'd been juggling as I had carried out my fugitive escape, I had missed she'd been losing condition and that she'd been feeding solely on the treats I'd been sharing out sparingly.

My gorgeous girl, my more-dog-than-chicken who wanted nothing more than to be by my side whether we were shipping parcels or doing stock takes and who barely ever made a noise, who followed my every step when I came home from a food shop and put 203 items away in the cupboard.

For four nights Lady slept in my kitchen, doing her best to race to greet me each morning even when her legs wouldn't carry her. I was still on my journey to discovering just how much love I truly had in my heart for my birds and now, of course, regret not spending more time just being with her as clearly my company was all she wanted.

It wasn't long before Cuddlepot got the broody bug again – I'd known that her breed was more into motherhood than businesswomen in an egg production world. So unable to resist her pleading looks and growls of protest at being turfed out of the nesting box, I order eight more Poland eggs to put under her and placed her in her separate housing again.

Egg hatching takes way too long and, as luck would have it, I had a holiday planned in the middle of it. It wasn't until I got back that I'd discovered my lovely pet sitter had felt that Cuddlepot should have the company of my other two chickens during the day, which caused them great delight as they took turns in laying their eggs under her.

Ever the dutiful mother she was now sitting on not 8 eggs but ten! With no experience in candling and a poor Cuddlepot who could barely stretch herself over them all, the hatch was a flop unsurprisingly as she'd struggled to keep them all warm!

But Cuddlepot was not ready to give up yet and neither was I, so off I toddled to a local farmer and amazingly managed to get my mitts on four new eggs for her. Quietly exchanging the ready to burst rotten eggs for her nice new ones we eagerly awaited developments.

As expected Cuddlepot delivered three rather gorgeous Poland boys! Yes, all boys – none of whom she could keep sadly, but all of whom went to good homes.

The following year Cuddlepot met my fiancé and quickly won over his heart, securing us permanent lodging rights at his home and soon his garden pond was replaced with a Cluckingham Palace as Cuddlepot had never seen in her life before.

Today our increased flock of 6 have daddy wrapped around their little claws, letting him know exactly when breakfast has not been delivered on time and commandeering the lounge on a wet day or wandering upstairs to find the perfect place to lay their eggs.

Cuddlepot retired some time ago from all duties except stealing hearts which she does effortlessly and continues to contribute to my ever-growing love, respect and understanding of these beautiful, underappreciated beings.

She sat with me through the writing of sixty-thousand words on cult escapes but has left this manuscript to one of last year's hatch – Noire, who mostly likes to try and eat my cursor.

Without a shadow of a doubt, all my birds have been essential to my mental wellbeing and my healing from the painful experience's life served up.

Today I write the inaugural book of the Fluffybutt Love series to share just how amazing and full of love these gorgeous birds are, adaptable beyond belief, giving and yet so undervalued.

Unlike the considerable investment a single puppy or kitten would set you back, chickens are very affordable and owing to that sad fact very few vets undergo proper poultry training, and historically just as few owners sought medical treatment instead chose to cull their birds, they are not given the full respect they deserve.

Yet chickens do not require long walks in the rain and will not leave your clothing and sofa's covered in fur, but instead will poop you breakfast faithfully for years.

That said, I do have one warning these little fluff balls that come in more shapes, sizes and colours than you can ever imagine have the uncanny knack of melting you into such an ooy-gooey mess and that any mathematical ability you have will be distorted out of all proportion, and before you know it, you will find your chicken addiction has exceeded even your wildest dreams!

Join the Fluffybutt Love Community (facebook.com/groups/loveoffluffybutts) to meet the owners of the amazing, feathered fowl in this book.

Find my Fluffybutt Love Facebook page (facebook.com/fluffybuttloves) which is run by my girls of course!

Submit your own story for inclusion in the next episode of Fluffybutt Love by emailing: hey@jessieshedden.com

*My personal Memoir **Tomorrow's Not Promised** is available at amzn.to/3kueDJQ and openly describes in detail my cult existence, escape and transition into the world I now know.

*Kind of white, because her white feathers had tiny black flecks in here and there making her look like she'd dirtied up her fabulous white wedding dress on engine oil as she'd hopped in and out of the car, which is want to hap-

pen on such auspicious events!

THE ORIGINAL FLUFFYBUTT LOVE

Sorry, I'm Late My Chicken Was Sitting on Me…

CHAPTER 1

HETTIE THE HEROINE

When I bought three hens in early 2019 the family's chicken math's kicked into action! Soon we had Skylines, Quail, Bantams and then we were fortunate enough to rehome some rescue hens as well.

Amongst our chickens, we have kept the last couple of years we had a home hatched Bantam called Hettie Spaghetti. She used to be with our main flock of rescue hens, heritage hens and home hatched chickens and she and her sister Amber would free range happily together.

After she battled a mutated respiratory infection in the summer last year, she lost the sight in her eyes so became a house hen so I could offer her food and water regularly - one benefit of me working from home mostly! I tried the positive and reward-based training I use with blind dogs and she learnt that when I said, "It's there." that the bowl of food was in front of her to peck at and when I said, "It's water." she would lower her beak slowly and drink.

Before introducing "Its water" she would throw her face into the water assuming it was food! I would also help her preen her feathers as she stopped doing it herself, so I gently brushed her with a children's soft toothbrush with colloidal silver sprayed on the bristles to help keep her clean, and she had eye drops from the vets to help keep the eyeball and socket clean and healthy both sides.

Hettie would come around the house when we were home and sniff about in the garden with the other chickens and with our terriers Merlin and Ripley. When we attempted to hatch ducklings only one hatched, which we named Echo, he lived in the same room as Hettie and they would lay together and communicate together in the garden, with Hettie showing Echo how to peck the grass!

Before Echo hatched, we had a couple of days away in our caravan and Hettie Spaghetti came with us so I could continue feeding her! She got to peck about in the enclosed garden area we created for the dogs, had her own pen inside, got to sunbathe, had plenty of food and even had some play with terrier Merlin!

She even sat in with me and the dogs one evening for a Canine Flow session which is like hypnotherapy online aimed at dogs and owners but as they said other animals can take part, I gave Hettie the option - she came in, mooched about, and when they did the countdown she actually stopped and fell asleep! When they counted up to wake the animal's Hettie woke up again and had a good stretch!!!

Our bond became so much closer when she was trusting us so much with things like having the dogs near her and little Echo who was running around trying to get her to play.

Sadly, we have lost her now, but she was fantastic to know and live with - she passed in her sleep an hour after I had been sitting with her in the sunshine.

I have continued using luring and rewards to work with all of my chickens - giving them new tricks to learn, interactive toys to play with to release food, and after my House Duck Echo became the world's first official Trick Duck in January 2021, I started teaching Ivy some tricks too!

Ivy is one of six rescues to come to us in November 2020. Initially, she was fine with her sisters in the quarantine enclosure. However, once in with the main flock Ivy was picked on so much, she stopped coming out of the coop for food or water and spent her days standing facing the wall to avoid attention. So, she's been living indoors for two weeks in a powder blue dog crate, with a sand bath and nest box and she comes out a few times each day. She's now eating and drinking, and she's not only healed but her feathers are growing back, and she is growing in confidence while she hangs out with Echo!!

Ivy has now started a few basic tricks and she looks to be enjoying them: twist, spin, peek a boo, and she's just started push a ball! This has all been happening while the

UK has a lockdown for the birds due to avian influenza so it's great that they can benefit from enrichment. For so many birds giving them something to play with and teaching them new things each day helps to keep them busy!

Joe Nutkin – Essex, England

CHAPTER 2

COMA CHICKENS

Three years ago, I woke from a 5-week coma, pretty much paralyzed from the neck down, on a ventilator and the world changed forever for this Harley-riding, tutu-wearing, taking the world on kind of girl. I was sent home only able to shuffle a couple of steps and to add insult to injury I'd lost all my waist-length hair too!

It was the 23rd of December 2016 and I felt dreadful. I'd been feeling ill since November, but I just kept plodding on. I drive to the big Tesco's in Bangor and dragged myself round, doing the big Xmas shop. I got home, fed my birds, unloaded the shopping sat down and posted to Facebook 'Please put me in the shed with my chickens and let me die'. I took myself to bed and didn't move again not even for drinks or toilet. On December 27th, I came downstairs and told my husband I'd phoned for an ambulance. Off I went to the hospital, I was desperately ill and so very, very frightened.

The next thing I remember was waking up in Feb 2017. Well apparently, I'd been "woken up" days ago - not that I remember. My first memory is of immense pressure on my throat, being dragged about on a bed and a nurse telling me, "You've been in a coma." I could not talk due to a tracheostomy and being connected to the ventilator. I also couldn't move due to muscle wastage and I was *terrified*!!

And then that's it, you are left to deal with it.

Skipping forward I became so frustrated at the lack of help and rehab, and at being left in a room all day on my own, going mad worrying about my birds and my beautiful old dog, that I started threatening to sign myself out. Totally ridiculous really as I couldn't walk but I'd had enough! So, a doctor in desperation approved to let me leave ITU and go to a ward if I agreed to stay in hospital.

A physiotherapist came to see me, wheeled me to the gym, and parked my wheelchair at the bottom of a flight of steps and told me to climb them. This, I knew, was my one chance at freedom. In my younger days, I was a swimmer and spent years in training as well as kayaking. *Come on right arm, don't fail me now!* I pleaded as I dragged my body and legs up the steps using the handrails and pure anger and determination. I willed every ounce of strength I could find in my arm and I pulled myself to the top. Later the physio told me she'd been told 'There wasn't a hope in hell I'd climb the steps.' I went home the next day!

My family and friends were not happy any idea of a warm welcome home was not to be. Except for Gordon, my beautiful white peacock. When he stood there and stared at me and started shouting, I thought my heart would burst.

But I couldn't walk, I couldn't stand up from a chair, I couldn't climb the three steps to the kitchen. I couldn't dress, I could hardly lift my left arm or brush my hair, my right hand was numb with pins and needles. I couldn't do anything. My family was 100 miles away and I was left alone at home.

My poor husband had been looking after my birds all this time and they had played him up terribly. The peacocks refused point-blank to go to bed! But he was determined he'd keep them alive even if it killed him. So, once I was home, I started shouting "Night nights" each night so the Peacocks could hear me and they went to bed.

My drive to see my birds was everything. I learnt to walk with a walking frame, to look out of the stable front door, calling "Chickie, chickie, chickie!' at which they'd come running for treats. If you've never seen the waddling run of hungry chickens, flapping their wings for an extra spurt of speed then you've missed out! I cannot begin to explain how happy this made me.

Every day I tried to walk a bit more, I learnt to do the steps, with much crying, but I did them. I fell a few times too. Within a month I was outside with my walking frame, feeding my birds. My husband finally got his life back to normal, no longer having to go to work in the early hours so he could be home in time to feed birds and get them to bed early for the long winter nights!

Despite my begging, still, no physio or rehab arrived. So, every day, in the rain and wind I'd be outside with my birds. I started sitting on a wheeled walking frame so I could muck out a coop. Now I was low enough to touch them, stroke them. Different birds would jump up and sit on my knee. Even when my hands didn't work properly, the need to touch and stroke those fluffy birds helped! What I used to do in a morning now took me days, but I persisted.

When Kea my beautiful Labrador died, I saw no point in going on - I was trapped in a house, on a mountain. I saw no one, I spoke to no one, my husband was working 6 days a week and now my best friend has gone. I seriously considered giving up, I wanted to die, I wished I'd never woken up. My body was failing me, and I was struggling to get any help. I had so much pain and relied on masses of pills just to keep me mobile. But again, my birds helped me. They needed me as much as I needed them.

You see when a human is injured, no longer useful in the same way, you find out who your friends are. I found out I didn't have many friends after all. It was a hard lesson to learn. But animals don't judge you. If you forget words and names and cry with frustration, because you can't remember what a baby cow is called, they don't laugh or get angry because you get things wrong. They don't care your hands don't work and when all my waist-length hair fell out and I felt so ugly, they didn't notice.

They are insanely clever and adaptable. Smaller birds flying up into the bucket swinging from my walking frame. Bigger birds racing my trolley for food. I'm out there in sideways rain, snow, 90mph winds. Three-four times a day, every day. I've lost years of memory and I don't recognize or remember some people. I've lost a lot of my memories with my husband. He's my second husband and we'd only been married a year when my coma hit, so we are making new memories every day.

So, what did I do next? I joined chicken and farming groups and as I got stronger and more mobile, I added more coops and somehow, despite my husband's constant begging of 'No more!' I increased my bird family.

Little ones, big ones, rescued ones, angry ones and then I discovered hatching! My ultimate dream is to hatch a peacock, a son of Gordon. But when it is raised by me, he will let me pet him and cuddle him - all the things peacocks don't normally let you do.

During 2019 my kitchen sang with the cheeping of chicks. It was the best year ever! When Star entered this world, I heard this strange bumping noise coming from the kitchen. In investigating I found this egg rolling about in the incubator being propelled by a foot. Obviously, this is quite normal in my world, I can't even manage normal hatching!

I'm not fancy so don't have an automatic incubator. Which means (much to my husband's amusement and slight fear) I have to reach in and manually turn eggs three times a day. Which obviously includes me singing to developing chicks "Is there a chickee in there for me?" or similar, you know like using baby talk. One day I reach in to turn a peafowl egg and it literally vibrates in my hand! I turn it over to find ChickPea part hatched. My first pea baby on my birthday too. My heart filled so much that I thought it would burst.

So where am I now? My spine has become so badly curved I can't walk without my wheeled walking frame. The pandemic means I can't get any diagnosis or treatment, so I continue to force myself to walk every day. A lot of well-meaning people tell me I should cut down my birds, make my life easier. If I did that, I'd be less mobile. Birds are my physio, my reason to walk each day, my reason to keep on trying.

What's my quality of life? Well, I used to ride motorbikes, rally, dance in a field, tour around Europe. Now I'm shielding, sat in the house on my own, day after day, praying John doesn't bring COVID-19 home and eating my own body weight in pringles.

I can't go out, look at the sea or visit my family. But with eight coops, chickens, ducks and peafowl I have a reason to keep on going. When it gets too much I sob or shout, but there are only the birds to hear me and honestly, I can scream blue murder and not one of my animals cares!

Without a shadow of a doubt, my birds are my physio, my reason to get up in the morning, my reason to keep trying and to keep going. I'd have given up without them!

Wolfie – Yellow Mountain, North Wales

CHAPTER 3

WEEBLE'S WOBBLES

Back in 2009, I was involved in emptying a farm of their last 10,000 hens before it closed for good. It took us four months, but we rescued every single hen.

We saw every conceivable ailment and medical emergency known at that point in rescuing hens, and other problems that had never been seen before. A small group, in particular, stood out from the crowd, and I had them all with me for rehab, about 10 of them in total. Initially, they were all unable to walk, when they did start, they all started to walk upright in varying degrees, some a lot worse than others, my vet did a team diagnosis with one of the worst, and she said that they'd been so depleted in calcium, that their thoracic vertebrae had collapsed, then re-set in an S shape, leaving them deformed.

Two, in particular, were really quite bad, Lilian, who my sister had, and Weeble, who I kept. The rest were homed in small groups of disabled only hens. These two girls were so upright, that they actually leant backwards; they could only walk left in a large arc, their vent was now on the front, because of their upright stance, and they were very unique, but they managed very well if a little unconventional.

Weeble was named after the Weebles from a 1980's TV advert for a children's toy, who had the saying 'Weebles wobble but they don't fall down'.

Life was good, she lived in a large group of my own disabled hens, and needed very little in the way of help, just low-level housing and keeping warm and dry.

Weeble was soon to celebrate her first year of freedom, which we always celebrate, but I found her the day before her Henniversary collapsed in her bed, I rushed her to the vets in Cambridge, and I had to leave her there for tests and pain management. It took just over 24 hours and two avian vets to diagnose her; she had herniated through her abdominal muscle wall.

I was given only two choices, major surgery, or have put her to sleep, I rang everyone I knew with hens to ask if they'd ever had a hernia repair? The replies were no, no one had. The risks were very high, but I truly had no choice, it was put her to sleep, or try. So, I signed the consent form for the surgery.

After what seemed like a lifetime wait, I got the call that her tummy tuck had gone very well. She didn't just have a hernia, two eggs and a loop of bowel had also passed through this rupture, so we had to prevent her from ever laying again, and spaying hadn't been an option, as the hernia repair surgery was already a very big deal.

* * * * * * *

A year previously, after a lot of research, I had approached my vet about implanting hens to prevent them from laying, this had never been done in hens before, though it had been done in Cockatiels. My hen Sally was losing a battle with egg yolk peritonitis, (EYP) so we implanted her to trial it. Sadly, Sally died of EYP, so we never did get the full picture if the implant was going to be a useful option, but we kept it on the backburner as an idea, in case of another do or die situation, when it presented itself.

* * * * * * *

Weeble bounced out of her surgery like a woman possessed; she came home the next day, with a large train track of stitches up her tummy. She'd also been given the implant. We had no idea what to expect. How it would affect her, how long it would last, or even if it would work. I recorded every detail of her life over the next few months, she stopped laying straight away, she moulted, her comb shrunk, she went very yellow in her face and legs, and this continued for around six months. Then all of that went in reverse, and she was showing signs of coming back in to lay, so again, for the first time in laying hens, she had a second implant.

We started to see a pattern form, and a very rough guide was formed as to how long it would last, and the safety of repeated implants, and I carried on with recording every detail.

Weeble wobbled on for over five years and eight months after her rescue, having a total of ten implants. Her hernia surgery held up remarkably well, but it was never a strong repair, due to there being such a small amount of muscle tone in that area, which is why we couldn't let her lay.

Sadly, as she grew very old, her knees had turned arthritic and she had loose cartilage in the joint, making walking very hard and she was starting to fall over. Her hips were also weakening, so I had to make the devastating decision to have her put to sleep. She was one in a million, and the longest living ex-battery hen I'd ever had at that point, which was staggering considering she was profoundly disabled, and she'd survived major surgery, all thanks to the skill of my vet, and the lifesaving implant, she really has left an enormous legacy for other hens.

Mel Lazenby – Cambridgeshire, England

CHAPTER 4

KIWI

All who visit the farm for classes, private consultations, or just as friends, have all had a chance to meet the ladies.

My nine chickies are just as much part of our hearts, our family, and our home as our pups, cat, mini horses, and jungle chickens (two cockatiels and an African Grey parrot).

About a week ago I went to let my little eighteen-week-old hens out to free-range and my girl Kiwi was limping. She's an awkward mover on her best of days, but this was different. She tends to be lower on the 'pecking order' and as the girls' age, they get, well... like girls in high school.

Even though we have about six huge roosts they all push to spend the night on the top one, pecking their neighbour's feet to get them to jump down a rung or move. I guessed that is what happened, but we didn't know for sure, so confined her to a dog crate in the coop to allow her to rest it for forty-eight hours.

I couldn't bear to watch her limp around in the days that followed, so I made an appointment with a vet that was well versed in chickens. They did x-rays and the whole nine yards. After my bank account sobbed, we still had no concrete diagnosis. No breaks, no dislocations, no parasites, etc.

So, she was prescribed anti-inflammatory/pain meds, confinement, and supplements. She still didn't improve, and her mobility declined to where she could no longer stand. She would fall forward and hold the front half of her body steady with her wings. She wasn't able to get to food or water. I called the vet again, and she was totally stumped. The deadly Marek's disease could be the cause, but she was not showing any of the normal neurological signs associated with it. So, we were at a loss with an uncertain future.

The moment I hung up the phone I started searching online for chicken wheelchairs. I figured they had to be a thing since we had them for dogs, cats, and other small critters. And yes! They are a thing. But they are not cheap! So, I put out a request on my personal Facebook community for anyone who could fashion me a custom chicken wheelchair (I'd pay for supplies and labour of course). Within about 5 minutes my amazing client and friend Michelle, and her husband offered to take on the task.

Today we picked up quite possibly the coolest set of chicken wheels ever made! I mean she has special wheels for easy manoeuvrability, a comfy soft sling with adjustable heights, a custom 'beware of the dog' flag, adjustable feed tray and poop hole, all painted badass jet black. Oh, and a whole second, wider frame for when she grows (she's only eighteen weeks)! Jamie and Michelle outdid themselves this time.

We don't know if she will improve enough to be mobile on her own, this is her only option for now and maybe forever.

With some at-home physical therapy, she is now able to hold herself up for about one minute. She will move inside and be a house chicken if need be. This is only possible because of Michelle and Jamie's kindness.

The point of my Kiwi's story is this:

There is a lot of negativity out in the world, now more than ever. But...there is also this little chicken in a wheelchair who now has a new lease on life due to the kindness of others. Whether it's for a dog, a person, or a chicken it shouldn't matter.

Only kindness matters.

*****

Update Four Months Later:

She rarely uses her chair anymore. She can walk quite a few steps in a row with the help of her wings to propel her forward. She's gained weight, strength, and actually started laying! She loves warm baths, scratch (of course), and any of the fruits and veggies I send their way. She cannot roost, so we made her two special places for her to lay on the floor of the coop and we built her own little 'log cabin' in the coop for the extra chilly nights and for a safe space for her to lay.

Eden Zook – New Hampshire, USA

CHAPTER 5

OVENREADY

I started keeping chickens around four years ago by accident. My brother had an allotment, and he rang me one day to tell me that three hens had been found on an abandoned allotment and they were in very poor condition, I told him I would meet him and take a look. When I got there, I saw the most pitiful three birds you could imagine. I instantly did a makeshift coop, got them food and water and welcomed Hattie, Ginger and Dottie to the family.

From there word got around that I was pretty much a soft touch and when allotment holders got fed up with their hens (usually because they had stopped laying) they would come to me and ask if I wanted the hen or they would dispatch them. Obviously, I invariably said yes, and they moved in with the original three. I ended up with two huge coops which literally took over my poor brothers' allotment! I had twenty-five hens, five ducks and one cockerel. The ducks had been bred for food so rather than see them go to the slaughterhouse, I bought them, and they lived out their lives with me.

Over the years I've lost many to old age and now I'm down to twelve girls. Hattie and Ginger from the original three are still well and happy, sadly Dottie died a couple of years ago. Hattie is very much boss bird and the others pretty much do what they're told!

At the side of my brother's allotment, there was another owned by a guy who kept hens, he was going on holiday and asked if I would feed them. That's when I first saw Ovenready and my heart broke, she was completely bald and stuck in mud. He had 5 hens altogether and the conditions were horrific. He was away for two weeks and in that time, I rebuilt their coop and gave them fresh bedding etc. I provided food and gave them clean water as they were shockingly drinking mud. I didn't know what to do for the best. My first thought was to call the RSPCA, but I thought they'll just come along and possibly cull them.

So, plan B was to try and keep on the best side of this guy in the hope that he would hand them over to me. I messaged him and told him that as Ovenready was near to death could I take her? Thankfully he said yes.

She was so weak, and I honestly didn't think she'd make it, I syringe fed her, and got water into her the same way and kept her in the shed, as I knew if put her in with my others, she wouldn't stand a chance. She was so strong and slowly she began to recover, I thought I was going to lose her again a couple of times, once due to being eggbound and then she also had three serious respiratory infections, thankfully with antibiotics, she recovered. When the guy came off holiday, I asked him outright could I have his other four hens, at first, he said no because he was making money from the eggs but eventually, I nagged him that much that he gave them to me.

They were instantly given names and they are still very much alive and kicking. They are named Lady Coughalot who has been checked out by vets and there's nothing wrong with her, instead, we think the cough is more of a stress response. Then there's Princess Sneezepoop, who's clue is in her name - when she sneezes, she poops. Coughalot and Sneezepoop are sisters and do everything together. They're like two little old ladies!

Then there's Hollie, very gentle, but also timid. Next is Omelette, who's cheeky, silly and quite naughty at times, good job I love her! Mable, Betty, Nugget, Tikka and Masala had been thrown out onto the lanes for the foxes after their owner didn't want them anymore so in her words, she 'threw them away'. I spent days trying to get close to them and finally managed to catch them.

I used to live in Manchester and have recently moved to Yorkshire, my girls, of course, came over with me. They have a very nice secure run and coop and are allowed in the garden when I'm home and able to keep an eye on them. For some reason Ovenready started to come into the utility room, she wouldn't go any further at that point, the door was left open so she could join her sisters if she wanted to but more and more, she chose to stay inside. She will come into the garden with me but would always beat me back to the house. I guess she just decided she preferred it indoors. Gradually she started to get very confident, venturing into the kitchen, sitting at the table and more than enjoys sitting in the sink full of warm water. She teases my cat relentlessly and tries to bully her off her food. I don't think the cat realizes what she is! Having said that I don't think Ovenready knows what she is either!

She loves cuddles and sleeps in the cat carrier, I'm not quite sure how old this girl is, but she will be spending the rest of her days exactly how she wants too. She had a rubbish start with a tough life, originally being a battery hen, but she has her forever home with me as well as a very relaxed and spoiled retirement. I have had a traumatic past and to be honest, my hens have saved me, not the other way round. I was agoraphobic and suffered terrible anxiety and depression for many years. These girls have been fantastic for getting me through so much, every single day starts and ends with a smile thanks to them.

Thanks so much for including Ovenready in the Fluffybutt Love series, I feel like her little life is being acknowledged and that can only benefit the rest who are still waiting to be rescued.

Margaret Hope - Yorkshire, England

Behind every amazing woman is a couple of dozen chickens!

CHAPTER 6

BLUE'S BLUE HEART

Blue was a day-old hatchling when she came to me. She had been unceremoniously picked out of a peeping bin full of chicks, that were supposed to be Blue Copper Marans, from one of the feed stores in Fort Collins, Colorado. Blue Copper Marans were touted to be a rarer colouration and a breed that was valued by French chefs for the rich, chocolate brown-coloured eggs they lay. As my family was choosing names for the members of our first flock, we just kept referring to her as the "blue" chick, and the name just stuck.

We handled the chicks daily and watched as they lost their soft chick fuzz and began putting on feathers. While most of the other chicks developed the colours we expected, Blue began to grow white feathers peppered with light and dark grey feathers. We soon learned that her colouration was Blue Splash.

Though not originally planned, Blue became the only chicken in our flock with feathered feet. Being new, inexperienced chicken owners, we assumed that since the chicks had grown up together, despite their differences they would get along. However, as they got older and larger, they began establishing a hierarchy and creating cliques amongst themselves, like high school girls. Naturally, someone had to be on the bottom of the pecking order, and that someone was Blue.

We developed quite a bond with our chickens that first summer after our plans to build a chicken coop in the backyard took much longer than anticipated. To allow them time out of their brooder, which they were rapidly outgrowing, we spent a lot of time with the chickens as a family. We took turns scattering mealworms in the front yard and watching them scratch around to find them. We lounged in the hammock on the front porch, often with a chicken in our lap. We even started picking out one to take with us on trips to the pet store or the hardware store. Basically, we figured, anywhere a dog could go, a chicken should be allowed to go too.

Blue became one of the fast favourites to take on trips in the community. She seemed to enjoy going on rides in the Jeep and having random strangers pet her and marvel over how she could be so calm. On her adventures, we learned how many people had never seen or touched a real chicken before and how many people were apprehensive about her because they had been chased by their grandmother's rooster as a child.

Blue always dropped her head and stretched out her neck for people to pet, and she would make purring noises and close her eyes when they did a good job. She was an excellent ambassador for her species, and we began to develop quite a fan base at the pet store and Home Depot. In fact, several of the workers told us that they looked forward to her visits and were disappointed when Blue was not accompanying me on a shopping trip. Blue also got invited to go inside the lobby of our bank, had lunch with us on the patio at a couple of local restaurants, and went on a few trail rides with our four-wheel drive club.

Returning home from work each day, my first stop was always the chicken coop to check on the girls, replenish their food and water, and spend time with them while I drank a beer. However, one day, I rounded the corner to find blood drops in the sand of the run and Blue with missing and bloody feathers on her feet. I scooped her up and took her into the house to clean off her feet and assess the damage. The other girls had mangled her poor feet and underneath the blood was red swollen skin. "Looks like Blue gets to be a house chicken for a while until her feet heal", I told my husband. Little did I know, but that was the beginning of the transformation between a great bond and an unbreakable bond for Blue and me.

After spending roughly two weeks in the 'hen-firmary' having her feet tended, Blue was healed enough to be reintegrated into the flock again. I did a ton of research on how best to go about reintroducing her to the flock so that it would be successful.

I found that the most recommended way was to put

the hen being reintroduced into the coop at night while everyone was still sleeping. In theory, they were supposed to all wake up together and be none the wiser that there was a newcomer in their midst. However, right after having let them out of the coop for the day, they jumped right back in to terrorizing Blue and pulling the feathers from her feet. It was at that moment that Blue became a permanent house chicken.

Blue was our only house chicken for quite some time but did not seem to mind being in a flock with humans. I ordered diapers for chickens for her to wear while she had free-range of the house, and she began to sleep on a bed made of blankets on my bedside table at night. The beautiful chocolate brown eggs we were supposed to get from her never came, but she had already earned a place in our hearts and our home, though my husband jokingly called her 'The Mooch'.

She had a unique personality and the longer she lived inside the house with us, the more of her true self we got to see. She would chase the cats away from their food bowl and then announce her conquest by tidbitting loudly for us. Tidbitting is typically done by roosters, trying to show their hens where a tasty bug or other food might be. Any time I was out of her line of sight she would make noises to express her displeasure with my absence. If I did not return in a timely fashion, she would become inpatient and crow as loud as her little body could! She would lightly peck at my knee to request a morsel of whatever I was eating or if she wanted to be held. She made purring, trilling, bubbling noises to express her happiness or contentment and would wag her tail like a dog, holding it up high as she did. She loved taking naps with me on a lazy afternoon, snuggled under the covers, she would nestle her face tightly into my neck and fall asleep.

As she gained confidence in herself, we were able to let her free-range with the rest of the flock under supervision just in case there were any arguments. If another hen came near her, she would fluff up all her feathers, raise one shoulder and drop the other to make herself look bigger and more imposing. We would chuckle and call her "Vinnie The Mooch" when she did that. Her Rockstar status in the house caused her to gain so much confidence, that she began challenging the head hen, Violet, in the flock every time they saw each other. The fights they had were nasty and in only the few seconds it would take before we could break them apart, they both usually had earned abrasions to their combs or waddles. Soon, the remainder of the flock began accepting Blue's presence again and seemed to accept the fact that while they headed to the coop outside in the evening, Blue headed for the back gate to be let into the house.

By November of 2019, we noticed Violet seemed a bit less sassy than before, so she was brought into the house to live in the 'hen-firmary' until she recovered. Strangely, after Violet moved into the house, Blue stopped fighting with her. I do not know what exactly prompted the change, but the two became best friends!

They never went anywhere without the other and even began roosting on my bedside table together. They had many conversations in the evenings before bedtime and looking back now, I wonder if Violet was teaching Blue the things she would need to know for the future?

As Violet's health declined, Blue and the other hens took a bit of a back seat. Violet was diagnosed with salpingitis, an infection in her oviduct system, and her care required a great deal of time and attention. Sadly, despite the best efforts of our family and the veterinary professionals who cared for her, we made the difficult decision to give her the last gift we could and allow her body its final rest. It was in those final few weeks of Violet's life that my family and I realized just how much our chickens had come to mean to us and what extent, and expense we were willing to go through to see our girls healthy, happy, and whole again.

After a period of mourning, our family decided to pursue pet insurance for our entire flock as well as our dogs and cats. With the permission of the CEO of our insurance company, after explaining the difference between my pet chickens and "normal" chickens, he agreed to have a policy made just for my girls! It gave me peace of mind to know that if another catastrophic illness appeared, we would have the ability to weather the financial storm it could bring.

Not long after Violet's death in March 2020, I began to notice that Blue did not seem like herself anymore. Realistically, she might have been feeling poorly for quite some time, but my energies had been so focused on the care of Violet that I had not noticed the subtle changes in

Blue. Though she had taken Violet's place as head hen in the flock, she seemed to be doing a lot of laying around. Her preferred way of guarding the food against the other girls was to lay in the middle of the feed tray.

She became insecure about jumping on and off things, instead choosing to come and peck at my leg to indicate she wanted to be picked up or by making soft, melancholic noises at my feet. She stopped crowing and making purring noises when I petted her, and she did not want me to hold her anymore. With only the slightest bit of stress or activity, she started panting with her beak open, and eventually, I began noticing her comb and wattles turn from a bright red to a deep purplish-blue colour. Going places with me and meeting people, as she had enjoyed before, became too stressful for her and as she sat in my lap in the car, she would lay her head on my arm limply and go to sleep. She began developing pressure sores over her breastbone and putting on weight from laying around so much too. I also noticed that she seemed anxious and had developed an irrational fear of the dark and overhead predators though nothing in her history suggested that she should be afraid. Blue also began making strange squeaking noises as she breathed and normal activities like dust bathing made her tired. When she would eat or drink, she would choke, struggling to coordinate the act of swallowing and breathing.

As I began noticing her symptoms, I also began seeking veterinary advice for her care. Throughout her condition, she saw local vets and big city vets scattered along the front range. We had countless radiographs, ultrasounds, and blood draws to try and determine the cause of her exercise intolerance and cyanosis. Out of the numerous diagnostic tests that were performed came just as many theories as to what might be causing her symptoms: upper respiratory infection, heart disease, heart failure, obesity, blocked nasal passages, cancerous mass in her abdomen, etc.? We tried antibiotics, diuretics, heart medications, and a diet and exercise program where we did repetitions of wing flapping or running across the yard for a small treat. None of the diagnostics that were done seemed to help point us to a cause, and none of the treatments we tried gave her any improvement.

I cried. I cried out of frustration that we could not find out why Blue was having so much difficulty breathing. I cried out of guilt for not having noticed her decline earlier. I cried because I was scared every time, she went under anaesthesia that she might not wake up again because she was such a high-risk patient. I cried every time she had an exceptionally bad day, wondering if it would be her last. I cried because I loved her so hopelessly much and wanted to hold and pet her again but dared not for fear it would stress her out too much. I cried out of exasperation with the veterinary community for having so little knowledge of the chicken species. I cried about the ridicule I had received and snide remarks from co-workers and friends who couldn't understand why Blue wasn't 'just a chicken' to me or my family. I cried for Blue, seeing on her face that she wanted to be able to do things like the other hens, but just did not have the energy.

The last theory for Blue's symptoms was that an abdominal mass, seen on ultrasound, was so large that it was compressing her air sacs and her heart causing them to work inefficiently. My husband and I decided that it was time to seek a higher power with the Colorado State University Veterinary Teaching Hospital's exotics department. I asked that they do an ultrasound-guided needle aspirate of the mass in her abdomen so that my family would finally have a diagnosis for her and be able to make informed decisions regarding her care. Our thoughts were that, if it came back as cancerous, we would put her on "hen-spice" (hospice for chickens) and keep her comfortable as long as we could, but if it came back as noncancerous, we would inquire about having the mass removed which we hoped would relieve her of any further symptoms.

Dr D.R., the exotics intern, spoke to me about the results that afternoon. The good news was that Blue did not have a mass in her abdomen at all, so no ultrasound-guided needle aspirate was needed. However, after performing a CT scan with contrast dye, they had found what was most likely the cause of her symptoms, a PDA (patent ductus arteriosus). In simple terms, a PDA is a connection between the vessels of the heart that deliver oxygenated blood to the body and the vessels that deliver unoxygenated blood to the lungs.

Normally, this opening is normal in a developing embryo, and then it closes before birth or hatching in Blue's case. A PDA that does not close on its own allows oxygenated blood and unoxygenated blood to mix as well as increasing the workload on the heart and lungs. While the congenital defect is fairly common in humans, people, dogs, and even cats, it had never been seen or described in any bird species...until Blue!

Closure of the PDA, no matter the species, involves the closure of the connection between the two vessels so that normal blood flow pattern can be established. The larger the PDA, the more changes are seen in the heart and the more symptoms it will produce. Essentially, I had two treatment options; take her home and keep her comfortable until it was time to send her over the rainbow bridge or forge ahead into the unknown and hope that it could be surgically repaired.

From my standpoint, neither option was good, and I so wished that I did not have to make such a difficult decision! Surgical repair was a huge risk, to say the least! This surgery had never been done on a bird before and the anatomy of the chicken made it even more difficult to achieve a successful repair. In dogs and cats, they would do an open-heart procedure, but because of the position of her air sacs in relation to her heart, that was not a viable option for a bird. I could easily lose her on the table, but if we did not even try, I would eventually lose her to heart failure. Her decline seemed to be more rapid as of late and I am guessing we had approximately two or three weeks left with her if we did nothing.

At the end of the day, the surgery offers a chance, albeit small, for her to be able to live the happy, pain-free life that we wanted her to be able to live. I would hate myself if I stood by and did nothing, just watching her continue to decline. I would be devastated if I lost her during surgery, but at least then I would be assured of three things: 1) An entire team of skilled veterinarians would learn something that day about poultry medicine and the human-animal bond that may help someone else down the road, 2) I gave her a chance most people would not have the care, courage, or financial means to give, and 3) that never was there an ounce of my love and devotion I did not give my beautiful girl Blue!

I was able to meet with Blue's surgical team the Friday before her procedure and was very impressed with the amount of research and legwork they had done to prepare. The cardiology team had to order some specialized equipment just for Blue's surgery, and a plan of approach had to be developed that would give us the best possible odds. Originally, they planned on approaching the PDA through her abdominal aorta, but after collaboration between the exotics and cardiology departments, they decided that a reduction in recovery time and her anatomy would be better served by a different approach. Instead, they would use a vein in her neck to thread a catheter through her heart to get to the area and deploy the device to occlude the defect. Though this approach would only leave a small incision, which would greatly reduce her recovery time, it would potentially add other complications.

In birds, their aorta exits on the opposite side as mammals. This creates a hairpin turn that the surgeon will have to navigate with the catheter. Birds also have thinner-walled hearts, so there is a possibility of perforating the wall of her heart, which would also not be great. They also mentioned that if she has an internal bleed it will not be immediately evident like it would be if she was totally opened up. To mitigate some of the concerns about the procedure, the team had attempted the hairpin turn with the catheter on a cadaver and succeeded. They also wanted me to bring one of Blue's housemates, just in case she needed a blood transfusion.

That weekend, Blue was treated even more like a queen than normal! She cuddled with me, spent time dust bathing, basked in the sun, sharing biscuits with me at breakfast, and scratching about in the garden. A pretty good day for a chicken, I think. Though the scientist/former veterinary technician/nerd in me was very excited about the surgery and what kinds of advancements in veterinary care, it could mean for chickens…the mother in me was terrified I might be spending my last moments with her.

Finally, surgery day arrived, November 10th, 2020! Blue and Butters, her large Buff Orpington housemate, checked in together the previous day so that pre-anaesthetic preparations could be done before the big day. Her procedure was scheduled to begin a little after noon. The veterinary team had arranged for a member of the Argus Institute to be my contact for the day.

The Argus Institute provides emotional resources and support for pet owners facing life-threatening surgeries or end of life care. Erin, my Argus Institute contact was nothing short of amazing! She notified me when they started anaesthesia and throughout the procedure. She even sent me pictures and videos of some of the procedure, at my request. She listened patiently as I blubbered and cried about my nervousness and tried to justify my insanity over having such a procedure done on my chicken. After the occluder had been successfully placed, she celebrated with me over the phone and explained when to expect a phone call from one of the veterinarians. When the vet called, he explained that we were not quite out of the woods yet.

Blue had weathered much of the procedure well, but she had experienced some abnormal heart rhythms and, just as they placed the occluder her heart rate and blood pressure had dipped dangerously low. They were able to give her medications to stabilize her, but after having been under anaesthesia for around two hours, we could only wait for her to recover.

I visited her in the Critical Care Unit that evening, and she looked rough. She was propped up on some towels in an incubator that was providing her with supplemental oxygen and warmth. She heard my voice and tried to lift her head, but unsteadiness forced her to lay her head back down again. I stroked her feathers a few times through a porthole in the front of the incubator, but I didn't want to agitate her, so I didn't stay long. She had survived the surgery, but things were still at a precarious point.

They had told me that they would call if there were any problems through the night, but I called to check on her one more time before crawling into bed. When the Critical Care Unit tech told me she was looking more alert, I finally breathed a bit and was able to go to sleep.

The next morning, I headed into work early so I could see Blue and get any updates from the veterinary staff before I started my shift in the Clinical Pathology Laboratory. I was shocked and pleasantly surprised to see her up, walking around, and pecking at some layer mash they had offered her! They were able to transfer her from the Critical Care Unit to the exotics department for the day and later that night I was able to take her home! They sent her home with some medication for pain and inflammation and an antibiotic to help prevent rejection of the occluder that had been placed. They also instructed us to keep her isolated from the remainder of the flock for a couple of weeks and keep her stress at a minimum until her recheck appointment scheduled for two weeks later.

At her recheck, Blue did great! The exotics department repeated her CT scan with contrast and did an angiogram to make sure everything was functioning as expected. The occluder was still in the proper position and just as everyone had hoped, the vessels were starting to constrict around it. Her heart size had also decreased, indicating that it was healing and not working as hard now. There was no indication of rejection of the occluder and her once prominent heart murmur was barely audible! Two years of living with an unknown heart condition left her with permanent scars in her lung tissue and noisy respirations, but overall, she is so much healthier now and doesn't have to take any medications!

Blue, herself, knows nothing of her fame and contribution to the avian species. All she knows is that my husband and I cannot get over the healthy, bright red colour of her comb and wattles! We smile every time she purrs with contentment as we stroke her soft feathers. We marvel at the little things too; like how she can drink water without sputtering or coughing, how bright and alive her eyes are, how talkative she is now, and how she again enjoys snuggling up close and burying her face into my neck.

Now the veterinary community knows a congenital heart condition can be found and repaired. They also know now that the value of a "barnyard" chicken can only be limited by the love, determination, and possibly a bit of insanity of a chicken mom, the imagination and ingenuity of veterinary medicine, and the skill and knowledge of a group of world-class Colorado State University Veterinary Teaching Hospital veterinarians and staff!

******

Update:

Blue is doing amazing at home and has become quite the celebrity! Blue's story was featured on the Colorado State University Veterinary Teaching Hospital's website which caught the attention of several media outlets.

Since the original story, she has also been published in a Northern Colorado newspaper, on several radio station websites and talked about on morning radio shows and was featured in a People Magazine article! Her case has also made a significant impact on the veterinary community as an academic, peer-reviewed paper is to be published! Her case is also slated to be presented at an international conference for veterinary cardiologists in Italy later this year!

Sarah Seleta Nothnagel – Colorado, USA

CHAPTER 7

GERTIE THE ESCAPE ARTIST

I was nineteen when I first met Gertie, and it was my first-time getting chickens. We rescued our first trio of hens from Fresh Start for Hens, and we turned up to the collection point, queuing up ready to collect. As it was our turn, a woman walked past holding an incredibly squirmy, scrawny hen. "She's a right escape artist this one!" she said, and indeed, the hen had the most disgruntled look on her face. I looked at my mother and as if she read my mind, she said: "Can we take home the escape artist please?"

Gertie spent her 11 months of freedom causing chaos wherever she went. She'd escape over the fence to go play with the dog (and subsequently lost the girls their free-range privilege while the dog was outside). Her first five minutes back at home consisted of her landing on my shoulder and staring at me in absolute horror once she realized where she'd landed. She'd break into the house, bully the other hens, and was generally a little terror! I loved her to bits though.

She got sick in July, and we spent every minute of her last day together. She had a bubble bath, which she adored, and then we had a cuddle together while watching Frozen II. We had a chicken sleepover, and she slept in a cat carrier in my room. The next morning, we took her to the vets, and she was put to sleep, having had egg yolk peritonitis. Her sisters, Florence and Henrietta, are still alive and thriving, and I have nothing but fond memories of my scrawny, scrappy little hen.

Aspen Palmer – Essex, England

CHAPTER 8

HARRIET'S VILLAGE VISITS

When I rescued my first fluffy butt's - ex-commercial heavyweight egg laying girls my foster kids gave them Harry Potter names, a tradition we still follow, waited to see who matched for personality. (I vetoed Walking Dead names on the basis that I wasn't going to stand in the garden and call for 'Jesus'.) Harriet/Harry, Hermione, Ginny, Fleur and Luna. It quickly became clear that the escape artist was the head hen, so she was Harriet. Deputy boss bird was Hermione who was very organizing and never stopped talking. Hermione liked to supervise and provide a running commentary.

Harriet was pretty feisty from the start. The rescue volunteer was catching and boxing 'my' hens; some were loaded into cat carriers and two were put into a cardboard box with air slits in the sides – Harriet immediately forced her head out through one of the slits, eyeballed me and started complaining loudly and trying to squeeze the rest of herself out of the slit. Even though I didn't know much about hens then I remember having a feeling and saying, 'There's always one isn't there?'. She was the one.

Not content with their own garden of nearly half an acre to free-range in, Harriet quickly found escape routes into the neighbour's gardens and took her squadron with her. That wasn't so bad when they just wandered around the neighbour's gardens for a bit and nobody minded.

Then they progressed to pooping on the patios and furniture and finally re-enacting the TV program Through the Keyhole - 'Who lives in a house like this?' Time to add to the fence to stop pop through's, launch pads and flyovers and uninvited house guests.

Unfortunately, that didn't stop Harriet from going walkabout. She couldn't get into the neighbour's gardens anymore, but she could get into the open countryside and fields at the back. We never knew how she did it as she wouldn't do it in front of anyone.

Harriet could never remember how she did it either; so, she could never reverse the process. She would dance up and down on the wrong side of the fence shouting and hollering to be rescued. So, to start with we had to beat a path through waist-high nettles to go and get her and then managed to train her to 'walk the plank' provided.

To start with she stayed quite near the garden fence. As time went on, she explored further away and eventually I started to get reports of regular visits to other people in the village who gave in to her bullying demands for some nice nom noms. I had a treat call to get the girls into their run for their tea. Harriet was always missing but on hearing my treat call would immediately answer, usually very faintly at first because she was so far away, then frantically at intervals to orientate on my voice and in a panic that she was going to be too late and all the treats would be gone. So, you could always tell which direction she was coming from -sometimes she was way out in the fields and sometimes in the village - as the 'Wait for me!' calls got louder and louder and closer and closer until you could see the long grass tremble as she scurried along at full pelt and eventually appeared, changing her call to shouting for her plank as soon as she could see you.

She'd then resume command of her girls, who would all be waiting for her, and lead them in for tea. Harriet even did this the night before she passed away with a heart attack in 2019.

Just sixteen months free and being a proper chicken. My neighbours and the village knew instantly as they were no longer entertained with Harriet's afternoon 'Wait for me, I want some nom noms too!' routine. Everybody missed her.

Not long after getting my first hens, my husband passed away, aged fifty-eight, and those hens got me outside every day into the fresh air and did wonders for my mental health by slowly blossoming and regaining their own physical and mental health and doing proper chickeny things (like pretending to be dead when they're sunbathing, purring when they're happy (they really do), and doing Benny Hill style chases when one of them has a worm or a frog, with me in hot pursuit in my PJ's if it's a frog.

They now live in harmony with my four cats, two young Labradors, foster kids and my two toddler granddaughters who love collecting the eggs and giving the hens some corn just like Peppa Pig does with her Nanny.

Nicky Dawson – Norfolk, England

CHAPTER 9

THE INVINCIBLE POP

On our allotment, there are many different chicken keepers. Some, like us, keep chickens as pets with the added bonus of the occasional egg. Others keep them solely for eggs and regularly rotate their flock. On our allotment site, we are known as Chicken Rescue Central. A friend who was wanting to try a different chicken breed offered us five of his beautiful Black Rock hens. I immediately said yes and a couple of days later, they appeared in our coop. The following story is about just one of those hens.

One day in late June, I noticed Pop was being pushed about more than usual by the other girls. After filling up the food bowl, I went back to Pop who was sitting where I left her. I picked her up and checked her over. She had some corn in her crop but when I put her down, she was struggling to stand. I tried giving her some food and she kept missing my hand almost as if she couldn't focus properly. Worried, I picked her up and put her in the nest box to see if she perked up after a rest. Later the same evening, I went back down to check on Pop. She was still in the nest box and looked around at me when I opened the lid. She still was very unsteady on her legs, so I put in a handful of food and a small container of water with cider vinegar. I waited for about a quarter of an hour, watching to see what she would do. Pop found the water and took a few drinks then had a go at some of the food. The next morning, I opened the nest box to find she had vanished!

Previously, the absence of a chicken usually meant a kind neighbour had spotted the dead chicken, removed the body and buried it for us. Imagine my surprise when I opened up the other nest box to find Pop alive curled up in a corner! I turned her around and noted she was still rather wobbly on her legs. Picking her up gently, I checked her crop which was mainly empty except for one spot where I could feel some corn. Just in case Pop had sour crop, I massaged her crop to encourage any blockages to shift.

Next, I found a small container and filled it with water. Pop ignored it initially until I put her beak in it. Over the next ten minutes, she drank lots of water and seemed to perk up a little. I went off to hunt for another container to put some food in, giving her a mix of sunflower seeds, pellets and corn which she wasn't hugely interested in and refilled her water which was pretty much empty.

The next week found Pop looking a little perkier, sitting half out of the nest box. Whilst my husband fed the girls their treats, I watched Pop take several drinks from her fresh water and even have a half-hearted peck at some food. Her crop was still empty and there is no apparent lump to indicate sour crop. Due to struggling to move, her rear end was a little mucky, but I cleaned it up as best I could. The following day I found her much more alert and compos mentis with a full crop and to top it off, she was holding herself up better. Pop still struggled to stand but she was able to push herself upwards on her hocks. I put her down in her favourite sunbathing spot and fed the others.

Two weeks after Pop became unwell and I was surprised to find she had managed to shift herself several feet forward out of the nest box. She wasn't moving in a very dignified manner (wobbly and with much use of her wings to help her move forwards) but it was a considerable improvement on not being able to move at all! Gently, I placed her back in the nest box, topped up her food which she had a good go at and put in fresh water. Each day I had been lifting her out of the nest box in the morning, putting a supply of food and water within beak range, and left her to enjoy the sunshine. Later in the evening, I would walk back to the allotment and put her into the nest box with the others. Although it sometimes is a hassle to go down twice, Pop really seemed to benefit from spending time outside with the other girls. They didn't seem to pick on her or bother her in any way. Her rear end wasn't as mucky as it had been because she was able to raise herself up and shuffle forward to keep herself from sitting in it.

Unfortunately, in the third week after Pop became unwell, our cockerel started to pick on her. I had to repeatedly chase Tommy away. She was clearly struggling to move so I picked her up and placed her in the small nest box with her food and water to give her a break. Later when I got back into the coop, I looked for Pop in the nest box. She wasn't there. How could she not be there?! Pop is barely able to shuffle forwards, how on earth had she moved out of the box on her own? After a few moments of frantic searching and I found her in the corner of the central part of the nest box. Heaving a sigh of relief, I placed the now cleaned boards back in the nest box and added a thick bed of fresh shavings. As I was finishing up, I heard a huge amount of clicking and squeals from Pop. Rey was sitting on top of her, attacking her. Poor Pop. It really wasn't her day.

I grabbed Rey and tossed her out of the nest box, picking up Pop and holding her for a bit to calm her down. With Pop being increasingly bullied, I removed her and put her into the greenhouse to give her a proper break. Her legs weren't as strong as they were a few days ago which were a serious cause for concern. Over several days, Pop seemed to struggle more and more. She was spending more time asleep and doesn't seem to have attempted to get up on her legs as much as she was even the day before.

Remembering that she perked up after having a bath a few days ago, I dashed home and came back armed with hot water. I poured all the hot water into a plastic box and topped it up with cold water and Epsom salts.

Pop wasn't happy about me picking her up today. I checked her crop which had some food in but not as much as I expected. She had a soft belly so no obvious signs of being egg bound either. As soon as I put her in the bath, she relaxed. I helped her uncurl her feet properly and sat watching her having a doze in her bath. After about fifteen minutes, she stretched herself and managed to stand up fully albeit briefly. Ten minutes later, I took her out and wrapped her in a towel to dry her off. This attempt to dry her was greeted with a display of disapprobation and as soon as I got the worst of the wet from her feathers, I put her back into the nest box with some fresh food and water.

Several days later, on a warm mid-summer evening, I found Pop and her new friend Leia happily relaxing together. With a bit of encouragement, Pop spent a good ten minutes picking through the food bowl for corn and even managed some small bits of weed. The problem of Pop not being able to walk increasingly worried me. She was beginning to eat more and although her depth perception was still off, she was learning how to locate the food faster.

So, after some online research and browsing of an Australian webpage, I discovered chicken wheelchairs are actually a thing! Unfortunately, the only place I could potentially order one for Pop was in Australia and they weren't posting to the UK during the pandemic. Undeterred, I asked on a chicken forum whether anyone else knew about wheelchairs and whether they worked for chickens. According to the replies, they do as it allows the chicken to retrain their legs without having to support their own weight.

One lady, who had the same symptoms as Pop, said she had taught her chicken to learn to walk again. Others recommended vitamin supplements which I ordered. What followed was a busy day, armed with a saw, a sewing machine and wildly optimistic confidence in my building skills. Sewing the sling was difficult and took hours – I am by no means competent with anything other than the simplest stitches! But finally, I had something which I was reasonably confident would hold Pop's weight safely.

At the allotment, I placed the wheelchair on a flat slab next to our greenhouse before getting Pop out. She didn't appreciate being held, nor having her legs put through the leg holes. But after a few minutes, she seemed to work out what was happening. Initially, she wouldn't put her feet out flat, keeping the toes curled in. I helped her get her legs under her and flattened out her toes. I kept having to put them out flat as she curled them as she shuffled her weight from one leg to the other. But eventually, she stopped. Feet flat and looking around, she seemed quite pleased with herself. I checked the height of the frame and was pleased with the fit for her. After being clucked at in a disgruntled manner, I went to get her food bowl and using an upturned plant pot, put it in front of her so she could eat. What followed was a happy half an hour of digging through the food and having a good look around her. As the sunset began to fade into dusk, I put her back in the nest box and packed away the wheelchair for another day.

The next couple of days saw Pop build up her time in the wheelchair. Much to the eternal amusement of the other plot holders, who walked down the central path, were amazed to see Pop sitting there like a Queen in her chair. Her toes were getting better at turning out although she definitely is weaker in one leg.

An added difficulty for Pop is that her legs had scaly mite. Luckily, there is a quick and easy cure. Most chicken enthusiasts use a thick layer of Vaseline to smother the mites and soothe the irritation. One of the guys on site has discovered a much more effective treatment which we now all use – Sudocrem. My friend kindly helped me put a thick layer on Pop's legs, rubbing it in between the scales to get rid of the mites. Over the next couple of days, the raised scales will fall off and the skin will be revealed below. Two applications over a week should see her legs all shiny and new.

I knew that Pop has a soft spot for dandelion leaves, so I went looking for some. Pop had begun to eat well, still preferring corn to layers pellets but also now adding greens to her diet. The amount she is eating was increasing and her depth perception fractionally better. Half an hour later, I looked up and saw her preening her feathers. Keeping her feathers clean and tidy was another good sign that she is happy.

But one morning, Ninja chicken made an appearance. There was the wheelchair, exactly where I had left it. There was the food bowl in the right place, sitting on top of the upturned plant pot. And there was Pop sitting underneath the wheelchair looking rather smug. How on earth she had managed to get out of the chair and crawl underneath it is absolutely beyond my comprehension. This was a chicken who could barely stand, who hadn't walked in over seven weeks but who can levitate out of a wheelchair! It's rather impressive although I can't deny being a little miffed that she has already worked out how to escape from the chair. I spent quite some time trying to work out how to add some sort of strap to stop her from getting out.

Two weeks after being in the wheelchair for around an hour a day, with only a tiny bit of support under her crop, she managed to fully stand for a minute. Whilst it didn't seem a big achievement, it was the first time she stood independently in weeks and although she couldn't maintain a standing position for long, it gave me hope that she would regain the use of her legs. That evening, when I came to put her back into the nest box, I found Pop had taken herself to bed showing she was increasingly mobile.

In the morning, I spotted her attempting to stand fully upright. It was extremely wobbly, and she didn't manage to hold it for long, but it was progress! The question now was, how long would it be before she could stand on her own for longer.

Just as she was showing signs of standing and walking, I had to go back to work. Of course, the contrary bird decided this was the time to start to stand properly. By the time of my day off, there she was, by the front of the greenhouse fully on her own two legs! She had got herself out of the nest box and had walked the entire length of the greenhouse.

A few moments later, my friend appeared, and he caught me up on everything that had been happening over the past few days while I had been at work. By now she had moved again but for some reason, had half tucked in her toes again thus making it difficult to stand without wobbling. I wondered whether she would manage to correct it herself or if I would need to put her back into the wheelchair. Pop managed to sort out her feet and we watched as she took a few steps towards the food bowl. Before we left, I cut up some courgette and gave it to her. No chicken loves courgette more than Pop. She ate half of it by the time we had refilled their food and water bowls.

By the next week, Pop was increasing in confidence with her walking although she is a little lazy when there is someone nearby. After weeks of having food put in front of her beak, she has come to expect it. Sadly, Beak Service was no longer available especially when she has been walking for nearly a week! This was greeted with no small amount of disapprobation.

To help her explore more, I built a ramp to allow her to get outside into the outdoor enclosure. Leia instantly jumped into it and began exploring. Pop hovered for a while, apparently content to remain in the greenhouse. After an hour of looking at the ramp, Pop had managed to get herself onto the threshold of the greenhouse door. Refusing to use the ramp built especially for her, she half flopped, half jumped into the run. Landing with a bump, she ruffled her feathers and thrust her beak into the food bowl with a smug look.

Pop spent another six weeks enjoying her retirement with her buddy Leia. Unfortunately, she became unwell and passed away in October 2020. In her memory, I began a tiny business designing and creating customized chicken wheelchairs for other birds like Pop. One of my friends kindly printed out a gorgeous photo of Pop and framed it, leaving it in my shed as a surprise. Now whenever I go into my shed, her beady eyes look at me and remind me how amazing our hens can be.

Lizzie Harling – Cheshire, England

CHAPTER 10

THE PASTA PALAVER

All my girlies are named after dead aunties. Don't ask me why I just get these ideas. At the time I think we had about twelve girlies and there were names such as Norah, Dolly, Lena etc. There would have been a couple of Welsummers, who weren't named after my dead aunties, but they were born and bred in a mega-expensive footballers' area of the Wirral, so they had posh names to go with the area they were from. So, they were Portia and Hermione!!

A friend was looking after my girlies a few years ago and they were playing at being stroppy teenagers and wouldn't go into the run where they could be locked in. Ha-ha! she thought, so not to be beaten the next day she took a bowl full of pasta for them. What happened? She threw all the pasta down, the girlies all followed her into the run, grabbed the pasta and all legged it back into the woodland (a very grand name for a few trees!) with all the pasta and poor Lisa was left looking like Billy No Mates in the run. She was stood there for ages! Bless her!

Much to my hubby's disgust, I bought them a chicken swing and they never even looked at it, let alone sat on it. I then saw a photo on a chicken site where someone bought a child's xylophone and there was a video of all their girlies playing it. So, what did I do? Spent more money and bought one and now I stand there watching to see which one can bury it in the most soil!!

When I reminded Lisa of the story, she was helpless with laughter about it. She said she was stood there for ages, and not one of them would go back to her as they were too busy stuffing their beaks with the pasta, she had cooked especially for them!

Wendy Steele – Manchester, UK

Me: 'I need to get my life together.'

Also me: 'Or….I could just go sit in the chicken coop, drink milk, eat cookies, order more chickens and not worry about it.'

CHAPTER 11

CHAKA KHAN

I walked into my first animal swap a few years ago and a man there had this one chicken. She had a slight imperfection of a curly toe therefore not good enough for breeding stock. She was this little cute, black-feathered beauty and a Crevecoeur.

Crevecouers are a dying breed here in the USA and his breeding them is important to bring it back, so he sold her to me. I named her Chaka because she had this wild tuff of hair that reminded me of Chaka Khan.

Chaka was a normal chicken and lived outside with the flock until one day I went to go feed them and she was just lying there. I thought she was dead. I brought her in the house and for three days I nursed her back to health around the clock. Hourly feedings, cleanings, vitamins and love!

On day four she was wanting to go back outside with the

flock, so I brought her out. Well call me biased, but I think they were all jealous of her beauty. Within twelve hours she was down again and being pecked at badly. So back in the house she came.

She thrived in the house. She came everywhere with me; she would ride the Lawnmower with my husband, and she was just like a little child holding our hands (in spirit) as she walked alongside us.

About five months later this same man offered me some more Crevecouers. So, I gladly took them. Chaka was so eager to be by them as it's as if she knew they looked like her and she finally saw her beauty. We allowed small play dates to make sure she was able to get along and be a chicken again. It was going great. She loved them and they accepted her.

On her final day with us, we brought her outside and a few hours later she was gone. No signs of her anywhere. I'm assuming a hawk, or an owl came for her. But I truly believe that within the circle of life she lives on not only in our hearts but in so many aspects of the circle we call life.

* * * * * *

Another time I was offered a full-size standard Cochin pair a few years ago, the Roo was beautiful and he was *huge*! I was a bit afraid of him, to be honest. Here in Wisconsin, we get snow and storms and once or twice a year we have *snowstorms*. Now let me tell you about my house. On three sides there are farm fields and on the south side, there is a highway. So, with the help of the wind, we get all the snow, and we end up with drifts 8 feet tall.

So anyways, we got a doozy of a snowstorm and my poor giant Cochin Roo got his feathers on his feet wet right before a deep freeze that night. Unknown to us we were having what they called a polar vortex. In the morning I went to go feed them and his poor feet were rock hard solid and frozen. I brought him into the house, and we began a slow process of warming him and healing him.

At first, he lost one foot, but his will to live was just as lively. You could see the fight and spirit in his eyes. We could tell his injuries were still not doing well and he ended up losing both feet and his legs. So, my husband and I did what we had to do! We built him a wheelchair and he lived in the house as we taught him to get around and eat and drink.

Every Friday, my kids would bring home a snack bag from school and gave me the animal crackers. I would sit and share them with Albert and every Friday he would wait patiently for the kids knowing what day it was. For about 6 months he thrived and was as happy as could be.

He was the most gentle quiet magnificent giant I'd ever seen. One day I started to notice that spark leaving his eyes. He was no longer excited for his animal crackers and I knew. With tears in my eyes, I again did what I knew had to be done. I picked him up and carried him, a blanket and a bag of animal crackers outside. I found a sunny warm spot and we sat down, in the sun.

I held him and told him how much I loved him and that it was ok to fly again. He closed his eyes instantly and he found his new set of chicken wings. Chickens are just birds to some and just food to many. It is very seldom that we get to look into their souls and see that they are full of love, joy and appreciation for their humans.

And it's very few chickens that get to look into ours and mark their spots on our hearts. Albert and Chaka will always have a place in my heart as do all my chickens. But these two...man...they gave me a piece of their souls and took a piece of mine when they found their second set of wings.

Dawna June – Wisconsin, USA

CHAPTER 12

CARDIFF HITCHES A RIDE

We started keeping chickens back in March 2020 and with having children we decided to name the few that roamed around the garden.

I work for a telecom's company and was going to work one day and said to my wife "I'm missing a chicken. I hope I don't start going down the road and see a chicken fly out from under my van!"

Off I went up the M4 motorway into our compound at Cardiff and nope nothing showed up, so I carried on with my working day. When I got home later in the day, I was still unable to find my missing girl.

I then started a period of annual leave so my van stayed parked up. A few days went past, and I walked past my van and saw a pile of poop and thought 'That's strange?' but just carried on my day.

The next day I saw feathers in my bumper and said to my nine-year-old daughter 'Oh no look I think I've hit a bird!' so I pulled the feathers and they moved and squawked so I quickly ran and got my van keys and lifted the bonnet and saw that my little hen had claimed up into my bumper and become stuck on a ledge. I finally got her out and got her water and food as she had been there for about five days in all. When I looked down at the ledge she had been sat on and she had even laid eggs, what a great girl!

As she was nameless at the time it only seemed right that we gave her a name, like the others, so we did we called her Cardiff and she is doing very well for a girl that travelled around sixty miles up carriageways and motorways!

Dean Burton – Monmouth, Wales

CHAPTER 13

THE BROOM WAVING SWAMP WITCH

Our city had just passed legislation that allowed for chickens, as previously barnyard fowl were not allowed within city limits, so I got some chickens for my forty-second birthday, as I had been hoping to reduce my need for buying organic eggs, due to developing an allergy to something in commercial eggs. I had been leaning on my husband about keeping our own, and he always said no. I would tease him about it constantly "I'm gonna go buy chickens today," I'd say!

But then my husband surprised me by taking me up to a feed store some thirty miles from our city home. There they were in the discount bin, a dollar fifty each. We ended up buying the coop, chickens, feed, mealworms, bedding, and a chicken care kit to keep them healthy.

I picked the six largest babies I could, all ISA Browns. Living in the city meant we had to avoid roosters, and

ISAs are a sex-linked chicken, the brown colour guaranteeing it's a pullet/female. Most places won't let you buy a single chick, and they need friends, so since we were allowed to have three hens, I gambled that half would probably die from illness or predators and we figured our neighbours wouldn't care.

These six chicks were loved, spoiled, and named. Our neighbours kept a watchful eye on them and would call me if anyone got out or anything happened. We eventually moved south of the city, to an acre in a township that allows you to have as many chickens as you want. They had always free ranged in the yard, and our new neighbours were happy to see the birds free and doing their thing, so we didn't need to contain them on a partially fenced in lot. However, we were near a creek and Lake Erie, so there are a lot of predators like hawks and eagles flying around. For months, my chickens managed to hide whenever they heard warnings from the wild birds about hawks, we knew free ranging was a risk, but we'd rather have them free and happy than have to buy expensive organic feed and shut them in.

One day, my favourite hen was killed by a hawk. I caught him on top of my feathered friend and ran out, heart in my stomach. I picked up my still-warm bird that chilly December afternoon and was just devastated! My remaining five ladies (Ginger, Honey, Twinkie, Sleepy, & Chuck) were all in shock, hiding near the creek in the bushes. They didn't leave their coop for weeks they were so traumatized. I buried Penny outback and cried for days.

But while scrolling Facebook a week later, I came across a free rooster ad. I was interested, because in my mind, if I had had an extra ten seconds, Penny might not have died. I decided I needed a rooster!

I contacted the lady, who was an hour and a half away. I figured that distance was just not going to work. No one wants to go that far for a free rooster. Well, she had family in Toledo, and I'm just north of there, so she spoke with her husband and she and I started sending messages back and forth. She knew of my loss and all I was doing to deter hawks now. Well would you believe it, she and her husband drove over here and surprised me with not just the rooster, but two more ISAs. One of which was dark like my Penny was (I had sent her pics, so she knew!).

This rooster bit me multiple times while he was in quarantine, which led to a name change from Aspen to Charlie (after the Charlie Bit Me videos), and even though he bit me and came after me while in quarantine, I figured he'd be better once he could free range again. I told him I understood the frustration after our own quarantine all of 2020!

So here I am with my new rooster and the first week after quarantine, he's out by the back door *growling*. I am a hot mess, having just grabbed a coffee, hair all wild. I mean I never had a rooster before, y'all. I didn't know they *could* growl. So, I glance out the window and see a *Bald Eagle* in the trees out front. *A. Bald. Eagle* if you please!

I run out with the broom, barefoot, in January, nightgown on, hair flying, waving a broom around and making what can only be described as a guttural roaring noise to convince our "symbol of freedom" that *my* yard isn't the place for an easy meal, to say it was a little PTSD-driven rage would be accurate!

It flew off. Thank God! But I don't know what my plan was supposed to be! Wave a broom at a *Bald Eagle* if it decided to attack? Like... Stopping this thing is a literal *Federal Offense*... Now I find myself I'm out there barefoot, near an I-75 on-ramp, and busy road, and I still need to get back inside past the (human aggressive) rooster who just saved hens who haven't given him the time of day yet! Thank God I had the broom! And that the one neighbour had already gone to work.

E.V. Dawson – Michigan, USA

CHAPTER 14

BIRDA'S BRILLIANCE

Let me tell you a story. I had an Ayam Cemani hen named Birda that had just had babies. She had been sitting on them at the barn and one *night* (our chickens absolutely don't travel the yard at night) she came to the house up the stairs to my bedroom French doors and was yelling.

I thought I was dreaming but finally woke up and looked out the door. Once she saw me get up, she went running back through the yard back to the barn.

I went running after her in a t-shirt barefooted with a cell phone light out to her nest box and there was a snake in there eating her babies! She had come to get me!

I got her some new chicks and put them in a little pen when I brought them home and she sat on top of the kennel like she was asking if these were her babies.

I was amazed. No one can tell me hens are stupid.

Wendy Rurak – Alabama, USA

CHAPTER 15

TINY TIM

My name is Marion Petersen, and I am a small hobby farm owner in southern California. I grew up on a large ranch in the San Pasqual Valley, California where I lived amongst over forty head of bison, ten horses, many ranch dogs and barn cats, and of course chickens. I would have to be honest when I say that I never really gave the chickens much attention. My days were filled with horses and animal chores or exploring the eighty acres we lived on.

Nowadays I live on two and a half acres, a scaled-down version of the ranch that built me. I still to this day have horses, goats, dogs and of course, chickens. I have always owned large chickens for eggs to eat, never for companionship. But one day while browsing farm animals on Instagram, I noticed a super tiny little chicken, which I discovered was a Serama! It blew me away at how tiny they are! My first thought was how would I get my hands on one? I searched high and low for a couple of Seramas to have. I was able to finally find a breeder about an hour away from me, so I immediately set an appointment to go view the ones she had for sale.

I showed up at this kind ladies house, and there he was, he was so small, pure white, with the most yellow-coloured little legs and beak, and his comb was perky and bright red. He was the cutest tiniest thing I have ever seen! He was so social and snuggly, as his breeder held him often. What I came to find out later, is that Seramas are the puppies of the chicken breeds. They are so very social. They imprint on us humans so easily, especially those whose energy resonates with animals.

See, I had never really had a small animal as a companion, except for a cat when I was young. But I watched this tiny creature engaging socially with me and the lady who sold him to me, and I was just blown away, it seemed he knew how to give hugs on cue! Who was this tiny little rooster?

Of course, I had to take him and a little hen home. I cradled him the whole way home. It was as if this little guy could sense what a hard time I had been having emotionally in life. I spent a day with my new friend before deciding to name him Tiny Tim. Timothy, when he was naughty! He rarely was though of course.

It was winter and chilly even for sunny California, so I worried that Tiny Tim would be too cold outside, so the obvious solution was to bring him inside and snuggle! I got a baby blanket and a basket and hoped it would be a good way to contain the poop. I wrapped Tim up in the baby blanket simulating mamas wing, He immediately snuggled into the blankie and fell asleep! He was just like a puppy, falling asleep in their bed. And so, this became routine for him and me. This routine started to last all day, where I was, Tim was. Tim loved car rides in his basket, he loved trips to our local feed store or a friend's house. We were always together.

I realized that I could not be Tim's only friend and companion, I knew he needed a real chicken friend, Maybe even a lady friend! So, I started the hunt again to find Tim a mate. We settled on a tiny little straight feathered Serama hen named Maye. Tim loved Maye, and me still, of course, But Tim was still the only one who came inside the house every day. I would go get him in the morning before I drank my coffee, I would bundle him up in his favourite blankie and we would snuggle. I then would let him perch on our counter and let him have treats. We did this every morning and almost all evenings.

Springtime arrived several months later, and I saw that Tim and Maye were doing the rituals of breeding, and I knew babies would happen soon. I let Maye hatch four eggs, she produced one boy and three girls! I sold the little boy and kept Opal, Pearl and Seraphina. What treasures they were and are. I had no idea how I got so lucky. Snuggling them was my joy.

Two years later one summer day, I put another small rooster in with Tim. I knew I was just gonna be gone a brief moment. But that brief moment became tragic. I came back to Tim and this other rooster fighting, and Tim had a broken leg. He began living in the house full time so that I could help him with eating and making sure he could get to the water. I changed his splint and bandages daily, which he was such a champ about.

But after a few months, we could see that it was healing as it should have by now. I searched all the options on how to let him live as comfortably as possible, in the end, we chose a wheelchair. In fact, another chicken mama and her husband made him one. Even though he was in the wheelchair, he still couldn't get along by himself. It became a full-time job tending to his every need, and I was happy to do it. I adored Tim so much.

Sadly, five months into his new life in the chair, Tim got a blood infection from living a sedentary life. It started in the joint of his bad leg. Knowing he was suffering, I rushed him to the vet where they confirmed my worst fear for him. I got to hold my sweet boy for ten more minutes before that would be the last breath he took. He passed on to the next dimension in my arms, his wings flapped open as his little spirit left his body, as I felt him go.

I won't go into the details of how I had a full-fledged panic attack after in the office, or how they had to wheel the oxygen into the room where I was cradling his limp body, as it hit me, I would continue in this life without my sweet Tim, my sweet ball of joy.

You see, big or small, grief is a crazy thing. It completely took my breath away. I spent time with his little precious body and decided to have him cremated. I wanted to take him home and make sure I could be near his energy and physically still have a connection to him. Tim came home on August 20 of 2020. I picked him up in the tiniest little wooden box that was no bigger than my hand. There was a small gold plaque with his name on it, and carved flowers on the lid. Enclosed also was an imprint of his claw, which was an absolute surprise for me. I burst out sobbing in my car, there he was, all that I had left of my precious love. I drove home weeping and wiping the tears away to ensure I could see the road.

It wasn't till much later that I could think of my precious Tim and smile, every memory was just so painful.

Three weeks after Tim passed into the next life, I received a phone call from a friend of mine who also has Seramas. She stated that she saw a little guy like Tim that was in a bad situation and needed some love and TLC, my heart sank. I was a raw wound that was wide open. I could not even fathom losing this little guy too, because he was in a dire situation. Against what my heart said, I picked him up and came to find out that the breeder who had him had not been good to him. He was malnourished, he had scaly mites and regular mites. Worst of all, the breeder had drilled his little spurs down to a bloody pulp. He weighed just 9.5 ounces, again, I'll save you the gory details of his recovery and mine.

It's been six months since Sonnie came to me that day such a mess. We were both broken and bleeding from different wounds, just two souls needing the love one another had to offer. Sonnie, my "sunshine". I'll have you know that without a shadow of a doubt my sweet Tim orchestrated this union with Sonnie and me. I feel Tim so close he used to make this sweet, long squeal when he was snuggling with me or in his favourite blanket, it was always music to my ears. I've never heard another rooster do it.

Well until Sonnie that is. He does the exact same happy squeal when I snuggle him or wrap him up in his favourite blankie. See, energy cannot be destroyed, we are electromagnetic beings, and we will always be. I know that Sonnie makes those precious sounds when my Timmy is near, and my mama's heart soaks in the love of her boy's. We can make such beauty from the ashes if we let love back in.

Marion Petersen – California, USA

THE ORIGINAL FLUFFYBUTT LOVE

My owner wants a garden and free-range chickens... Hahahahahaha!

CHAPTER 16

TAILLESS TUCTUC

In May 2020 our little Poland boy TucTuc was hatched from eggs purchased off eBay by our friend. It was the first time we'd kept chickens and I still remember the message saying, 'One of your chicks is a right bossy little number!'.

He was running with another thirty or so youngsters at the time I collected him and the other chicks when they were ten days old and was informed that he had a pasty butt. But that was nothing unusual for tiny babies. So, ever since I've been religiously cleaning him and trimming his feathers. He's twenty-four weeks old now and we are still at it.

You see he was born with a birth defect - no tail. This means he soils himself. Most people would have culled him by now, but I just haven't got the heart to. He's so happy and does a wing dance for me every time he sees me. He brings his girls up to the backdoor and waits for me to come out for hours. He crows if he hears my voice inside and tries to get us to go to bed with him in a coop every evening.

I've been advised that his mucky rear end could cause infections to the hens when they are ready to be treaded. But he's here at the moment and we are making the most of it. There'll never be another TucTuc.

I have rehomed two of his healthy brothers but decided to keep him as he's such a wonderful character and he is currently in charge of nine girls of various breeds. It seems that as long as I'm keeping him clean everyone is healthy and well so far, so I'm glad I didn't get rid of him.

Virginia Hill – Caernarfon, North Wales

CHAPTER 17

POSSUM PLAYS DEAD

Let me tell you a funny story about one of my Silkies, who can play dead. My Dobermans, having extremely high prey drives, will torment the chickens if they are out at the same time. Which obviously we never do on purpose, but I do have two sons with autism, so it has happened occasionally. Anyway, the Dobermans don't bite them, but they will pick them up and bring them to us.

We found out because Stella, our oldest Doberman, brought one to my husband while he was at the barn.

He, of course, told her to drop it, being scared to death that she had killed it because it was limp and lifeless looking. When she gently laid it down, the poor thing must be all feathers, because it looked like a drowned rat.

So, he took Stella inside and came back to get the chicken, and then just as he walked around the corner, the chicken stood up, looked around and started strutting away like it had won the fight!

Connie Sides – Alabama, USA

CHAPTER 18

YOGI BEAR

As a dog mom, when I hatched our ten Poland baby chicks, I was slightly apprehensive at letting Yogi our Airedale Terrier out around them as Airedale terriers have a natural instinct to hunt and he loved nothing more than to chase rabbits, pheasants and anything that ran, but he was grand! For some reason, he was protective of my Poland flock. My birds took an instant love reaction to him and from then on, I trusted him to look out for them.

He loved to sit with them all out in the sunshine and allow all ten of them to jump all over him. Sadly, Yogi passed away in March aged sixteen. All my Polands had names. Mumble, Uno, Frodo, Frizz, Lady fudge, Mr Brown, Memphis, Dude, Phillipa....to name a few.

Linda Eblett – Lockerbie, Scotland

CHAPTER 19

CLUMSY CAMILLI

I realized I had a chicken addiction after I hatched some baby chicks. It all started off as just three chicks then before long, I had thirty. Now I only have twelve chickens due to having to move. However, I have to cuddle all my chickens daily and I love sitting with them in the yard.

Let me tell you about one of them in particular Camilli, who is the most clumsy, uncoordinated, fragile chicken ever. I remember the day I picked her up, I loved her instantly.

She is so funny. She's four years old, but when I rescued her two years ago I honestly didn't know how she survived. She's my smallest chicken, a little Belgian d'Uccle Frizzle. She's even a lot smaller than my other Belgian d'Uccle.

It was windy one day and I went to check on all my babies

and I see Camilli rolling around the backyard being taken by the wind! I rushed to her, picked her up and shook my head 'What are we going to do with you, Camilli?' I asked her. Despite being pretty solid for her size, she's so light, that I now have to make sure she's either inside or in her coop on very windy days!

Camilla needs baths weekly as she's so grubby, literally gets everything and anything on her, she's pretty much dark brown by the end of the week. She doesn't like her baths or the blow dryer. But she gets a treat at the end and always has a water beard after drinking water!

Camilli doesn't walk, she runs and falls over every time because she's going too fast for her little body. I've never seen a chicken run like that. It's like skipping, but on a chicken, she hop-runs! She can walk, but she just prefers to run, and her legs are fine. I've had her for 2 years and it cracks me up every time!

Camilli can't fly due to her wing feathers as they are like long pins. The weekly baths help with her feather growth. Her feathers are fine everywhere else just not in a couple of places on her wings. Camilli has been to the vet many times for check-ups and she's as healthy as she can be for a small little chicken.

She lives with chickens that accept her for her, if she's not happy with them she will let them know. She's small but mighty. She's the size of my partner hands or tall as a small bag of 1 kg flour or sugar.

* * * * * *

One of my other chickens is Sparky.

Sparky snuck inside one day while I was at work. The first I knew of it was when I got a text message from my partner saying he'd found a chicken in the toilet, what he should do?

I asked him to send me a photo and sure enough, there was Sparky, just sitting there chilling. My partner got him out and washed him the best that he could.

He wasn't harmed at all, as I believe he wasn't there any longer than twenty min's as I was arriving at work when I got the message. I just thought it was rather funny it made my day! I don't have Sparky anymore, but he went to an amazing home.

My girls are all very loved. They all run to me when they see me, and this makes my day. Animals are the greatest gift. They don't judge you. Instead, they are curious, kindness and able to sense emotion.

Bonney A.R. – Brisbane, Australia

CHAPTER 20

BIG BUFF MISTAKE

In May 2020 I advertised looking for Buff ducks and even included pictures of my ducks in the ad. It didn't take long for a lady to contact me and say she had two I could have.

Well, I jumped in my jeep and took off to meet her. When I get there, she hands me the box with what I thought contained the ducklings. With delight, I opened the box and lo and behold two 2-week-old chicks are looking back at me!

I looked at her quizzically and said 'But I was looking for ducklings...' It transpires she had no idea that there was such a thing as Buff ducks and thought that I had been looking for Buff Orpington chicks. Apparently, she didn't read my ad very well.

Needless to say, I had wanted to get chickens eventually, so this funny little misunderstanding has led to me having a flock of ten now (hubby says no more, but we'll see about that!).

I laughed pretty much all the way home because instead of coming home with ducklings I was coming home with chicks!

Stephanie Fincher Kelley – Alabama, USA

I only want ~~3~~ ~~6~~ ~~10~~ ~~15~~ ~~24~~ 48 chickens
Hey! Don't judge me!

CHAPTER 21

RUDY-RUTH

We decided to get our eight girls a roo, as they were close to laying age and we wanted them to be protected and eventually, maybe, hatch some babies of our own. Well, that and my girls were getting a little out of control with free ranging to the neighbour's houses!

I searched and searched until I found a lady close by that had Buff Orpington Roos and off I went to get one. When I arrived, she introduced me to him, bear in mind here I'm a fairly new chicken owner and told me they even called him Henry. We came home, renamed Henry, to Rudy, and started the quarantine and introduction process.

After quarantine, I let Rudy sleep in a dog crate inside of the coop to start introductions. The following morning, I went out to check on the progress and there was an egg in the crate. I immediately got excited and thought this rooster had encouraged one of my girls to start laying and that they must have gone and laid on top of the crate. But the more I thought about it, there was no way that could have happened, the egg wouldn't have fitted through the crate bars and it would have surely been broken during the fall. I sceptically looked at 'Rudy' and thought we'll see what the next day brings. The next day brought another egg!

Needless to say, Rudy is now Ruthie, and we have a new (true) Rudy! My six-year-old tells everyone we have two roosters; one is a boy and one is a girl!

Amanda Quire – Kentucky, USA

CHAPTER 22

HUGO'S HOTPOINT

We had a white Sussex bantam cockerel, years ago, named Hugo, who was a pretty perfect specimen.

We entered him in a show competition and the day before our next-door neighbour's cockerel, Hotpoint (they were all named after electrical appliances) escaped, came into our garden, and attacked Hugo. He pecked his perfect comb, sending blood everywhere.

I heard the commotion and went running out to split up the fight. Whilst the neighbours came over to retrieve Hotpoint, I collected up a bloody and bruised Hugo, who then had to spend the night in a box recovering and regaining his dignity, but his comb was sadly deformed forever.

His place in the show had to be cancelled and he was never re-entered. He was the coolest cockerel ever! He had so many adventures, he was even stolen by a dog once! I chased the dog down the road screaming 'Give me my chicken back!' while he was in the dog's mouth, luckily an old man with a walking stick, collard the dog so I could get Hugo back! He was a tough cookie!

Rebecca Robinson – North Derbyshire, England

CHAPTER 23

MOMMY V FOX

One summer evening I found myself rescuing one of my girls from an attempted fox attack.

I heard one of my girls screaming at the back door and looked out to find he had her in his mouth and was running off. I ran out in my PJs caught up with him, surprised myself by kicking him in the butt as I never expected to catch him! He dropped her and thankfully she was unharmed due to a little coat I'd put on her to help with her lack of feathers and stop her from being pecked.

She ran the length of the garden and into our house - totally scared, while her sister hen hidden under the little shed. I promptly dived into the house after her not wanting my house cat to A) escape or B) eat my rescued hen.

I find my hen on the living room windowsill, phew! I turn and pick up my terrified cat up, who scratches me to death and lock her on the stairs. I then dash back through the house to check on the hen that is hiding outside, in doing so I step on the kitchen tiles in damp fluffy bed socks and woosh I slip and knock myself out on the kitchen side and break my hand and wrist by landing on them.

After a brief daze, I call my neighbour over to help the hens to bed. He arrives wearing his industrial gardening gloves as though they were tiny-dino-killing machines and I then spent the evening in Accident & Emergency trying to convince the doctor my injuries were accidental, and I hadn't been beaten up. Chicken Mommy 1 - Fox 0

Clare Hinkley – West Midlands, England

CHAPTER 24

THE VILLAGE LOVE JIMMY

I brought Jimmy home from work, he was part of a huge clutch of eggs from one of our Pekin girls, he had three brothers, but they got to the age where they were squabbling, and options were running out for them as it was the middle of the first COVID19 lockdown. It was a very last-minute thing, so the day we got him I popped notes through our immediate neighbours' doors to let them know the situation.

After a couple of weeks of him living with us, a post appeared on our local Facebook 'shout out' page, one of our not so close neighbours was complaining about the crowing.

So many people ended up commenting on the post in support of Jimmy that I ended up posting our own post to introduce him and it blew up! Over four hundred comments from locals saying how beautiful he is, how they love hearing him and other cockerels around the town and nearby villages, how cockerels crowing are a part of living in the countryside... My favourite comment was from a neighbour we've never met who said that her little boy cock-a-doodle-doos whenever he hears Jimmy.

We had neighbours asking to meet him if they bumped into us in the street, my partner took him for an elderly neighbour to see him through the window and she commented how handsome they both were, partner, came back blushing!

When I saw the first post, I was so worried that the community would turn on us and Jimmy, but it was lovely to see so much support when usually you only hear the negatives of cockerels.

Emily Rose Thorp - Wiltshire, England

CHAPTER 25

A GIANT CHICKEN ADDICTION

When did my chicken addiction start? When I first got those baby chicks! For me, that was about 12 weeks ago. I contacted our local feed store about chicks. By this point the coop was underway, the broader was almost complete.

They told me that they had already placed the order however they would call me once they came in as they may have extras, and sometimes people don't pick up their chickens. They called 1 week later, so my boyfriend and I went to look.

I was *so ecstatic* that I really didn't hear everything the lady was telling me. Nor did I comprehend the paper she handed me with all the different breeds they had, with egg colour size etc.

What I heard was *babies*! "You are finally getting baby chicks!! You are going to have chickens!"

"It's recommended that you have a minimum of three chickens so if one dies, they still have another chicken. Though more is always better since they are flock animals and you almost always lose at least one if not a few." is what the lady clerk said.

I heard three of each *kind* of chicken and what's a few more anyhow?

3 Rhode Island red

3 Speckled Sussex

3 Plymouth

3 Silver Wyandotte's

3 Brahma

3 Black Jersey Giants....18 chickens later....

After we got in the car my boyfriend turns to me and says *"Did you listen to anything that lady was saying? Like about those three little black chicks?"*

Me: *"Yeah aren't they cute?!"*

Boyfriend: *"Jolene they are called Black Jersey **giants**. They lay XL eggs. They are going to be big chickens!"*

Me: *"Oh well we have the room."* (For like for literally forty chickens.)

Next day talking to a friend of mine who has chickens

and I told her what had happened and she's like, *"Oh well depending on what kind of Brahma chicks you got, you could have six XL chickens!"*

Oops!

I definitely did not research the breeds. I was in a state of ecstasy fulfilling a dream and totally went on impulse and cuteness! Though I now have desires for other breeds, like frizzles or Silkies.

I stopped into the store again 6 weeks ago and told the lady that all eighteen of my chicks made it! (Proud momma moment!) And then she says..." *We just got more chicks in."*

Me: *"Oh I think I am good with the eighteen I have, thanks."*
Clerk *"Well...these ones have afro's on their heads..."*

Me: *"Ok show me!"*

And that's how I ended up with three Poland hens!

*Side note I am back down to eighteen as I gifted three of my chicks to help a friend develop his flock after several of his died.

Jolene Kunde – Michigan, USA

I scream and scream until I get the nesting box I want!

CHAPTER 26

CHAMOIS THE SHOWSTOPPER

I've had my little Chamois Poland since I was thirteen years old and I raised her from a baby chick. She always stood out and became a firm favourite.

It was around the starting of my show career, that she won six different champion Juvenile awards for me at local poultry shows. As I got more experienced and better at showing and preparing my birds for the shows she continued to go through this great journey with me.

I am now twenty-four years old and still have her. She retired from her last shows 1 ½ years ago. She's won over a hundred and twenty first prizes in her show career. Including reserve breed champion at the Scottish National when she was seven years old. It's unheard of a chamois being so successful at this age. She was put forward to feature in the Poultry club book of standards.

She loved every minute of being at the shows and everyone would always say *"Wow she's still doing her thing, she's like the hen that doesn't age."* I am very proud of her. She is treated like royalty at my World of Poland's Stud which is based in the lovely countryside of County Antrim in Northern Ireland.

She always gets her daily treats of fresh veg and you can never go past her without lifting her for a little stroke. I hope she has many more years of happiness with me as I really don't know what I'd do without her.

Between the ages of eight to ten, she didn't lay one egg but last year she managed to lay five eggs, three of which hatched so hopefully they will carry on her legacy.

My great friend Jerry Logue who is ninety-three years old told me she was the greatest Chamois he has ever set his eyes on. It felt like a dream come true hearing this as he is a bit of a poultry legend in Northern Ireland. Little chamois also liked what he said!

James Weatherup – County Antrim – Ireland

CHAPTER 27

LOPSIDED LIL

My debut into chicken keeping started with Lily (aka Lopsided Lil, Lilybeth or Lily Lollo, depending on my mood), though sadly this is a kind of eulogy as she left us today, after an unexpected illness. Lil arrived in early April 2019 so had a year and a few days free, each of which was a joy.

I work as a volunteer for Fresh Start For Hens in rescuing ex-commercial hens and it was on one of our rescue missions that Lily was immediately noticeable as a 'special needs' hen so was whipped out of the transport crates and into our hospital wing for observation. She had a very strange head and neck movements, a little like Parkinson's might look. She was sent to see our specialist vet as a precaution. She got a very clean bill of health and Craig (our avian vet) thought it either a hatch defect or a historic brain injury.

Over the coming days, the extent of her lopsided-ness became increasingly obvious. Her neck regularly moved itself in and "up and under" movement so her head was on its side, which she had no control over. She walked like she'd been on the gin...a staggering diagonal no matter which way she wanted to go as one leg didn't quite work properly. She'd lie on her side with her weak leg sticking straight out to preen, she frightened us the first few times we saw it. She'd often lean her weaker side against a wall or fence for support as she walked, would run with one wing at an angle to help balance and would tire easily. Despite all this, she rose up the pecking order and took no sh!t from her flock mates. She was one strong-willed lady with a real fighting spirit.

She developed diarrhoea for no apparent reason a couple of weeks ago and didn't respond to whatever treatment we gave, although her attitude and fortitude shone through. She went to see Craig again today, for Xray and potentially exploratory surgery to find out what was going on. He thought maybe an internal abscess or pocket of infection could be the cause. The X-ray showed a mass in her abdomen but also that her organs weren't all where they should be. She was as wonky on the inside as on the out, it seems.

We made the decision to let her go, Craig wasn't confident that surgery would have a positive outcome or that he'd even find anything removable or treatable in there. So, for my beloved Lopsided Lil, I made the hardest decision and sobbed until I had snot bubbles while making it. This hen got to both mine and my partner Sean's hearts in a big way and took a chunk of them with her. She was truly loved and will be missed. Goodnight Lilybeth, you'll never know just how special you were.

THE ORIGINAL FLUFFYBUTT LOVE

Emma Mitchell – Leicestershire, England

CHAPTER 28

FLOCK BOSS

How I became a backyard chicken farmer: Back in July 2020, I built a beautiful chicken coop and run from a timber play/cubby house.

COVID19 had hit the world a few months earlier and I needed a happy project. I did lots of research and decided as I live in the suburbs, I should get some sweet (non-flying) Silkies.

I stocked up on medication & food and even made a two hour round trip to the Blue Mountains to buy some sweet-smelling lemongrass bedding so I could blend some lavender into it for a spa-like nest.

I bought feeders and an overpriced water tube because it was red & cute! I built a dust bath and placed a log in the run for chicken play. I was like a crazy expectant mother hen.

I was still too nervous to get my girls, so I killed more time building a garden around my chicken run, planted lavender, mint, lemon thyme, lemon balm and geraniums as I read that they deter insects. I even installed a solar fan and webcam in the coop and set up a rainwater tank to collect water off their roof.

I wanted everything to be perfect.

I was all set but petrified to actually go buy my girls. Luckily my husband pulled me aside and asked me if I was ever going to put some hens in the palace.

So off I went to this amazing breeder farm on the outskirts of Sydney and chose my three girls - Audrey, Selina and Laverne.

I can't tell you how nervous I was when I got them home. The temperature was in the forties and they all had their beaks open in the heat. Luckily, they settled in quickly and I became a real-life suburban chicken fancier with my own flock - well kind of!

On day two I decided to give them a spa day and I gave each one a bubble bath with baby shampoo and a blow-dry.

Laverne my youngest had some poop stuck to her foot so I decided to give it a little snip. I ended up snipping her foot and there was blood everywhere, all over my sink. I was in a panic; how could I do this to this sweet little girl? I had no one to ask directions of and ended up dunking her in a bowl of flour to stop the bleeding, amazingly enough, it worked!

This was followed by many tears (mine) and me checking on her hourly to make sure she was okay. The next day sleepy-eyed from my chicken foot disaster, I decided to be responsible and administer worming tablets to my small flock of three. Selina sadly hated me at first sight and even more so when I managed to catch her, and I threw the tablet down her throat. It then occurred to me that in my haste, it might have gone straight down the trachea into her lungs!

I'm now day two with two sleepless nights under my belt. At this point, I was thinking I'm the worst chicken fancier ever! And many mini were to disasters follow. But it's now January, my flock is intact, my girls are healthy and happy and all of us have survived cut feet, amateur pill dispensing, the dreaded broody, ramp falls, leaky roofs and a whole gamut of minor disasters.

At the end of the day, my girls are always happy to see me and they are the most fabulous, sweetest pets. I've learned a lot these past few months, but with all that, I'm now a 'ridgy-didge' backyard chicken farmer and wouldn't change it for the world!

Libby Downes – Sydney, Australia

CHAPTER 29

NUGGET

A while ago I learned about Seramas and found a lady on Craigslist selling some way outside of Portland and went and picked up a pair. Then they multiplied. Now I have...well.... maybe sixty Seramas? Not to mention the few that live indoor and free-range the house in diapers, much to the chagrin of my poor husband!

Often, I hear him muttering *"Chickens, everywhere I look, there are chickens."*

Let me tell you about one in particular – Nugget who originally lived with his hatch-mates, but out of the blue he started beating the heck out of them constantly, and I had no idea what to do with him. So, of course, I brought him inside!

I made a little perch for him that was attached to some shelves in the kitchen, and at first, he stayed up there and just watched everything that went on. He especially loved watching my friends and I play DandD.

Then, of course, he started flying off his perch, exploring, bossing the cats around, and basically taking over the house. He learned he loved to go for car rides and visit different places, including local pioneer cemetery. I could even let him out in a parking lot, and he would never, ever fly off.

He turned out to be one of my favourite chickens of all time, and now he lives in his own little condo in my hobby room with his two wives (who have popped out many babies, by the way). When I take him out to hang out with me, he gets so excited he can hardly contain himself! He tries to fly up on my head repeatedly until I've given him enough hugs and love!

Marissa Troxclair – Oregon, USA

CHAPTER 30

HAPPY HATCH DAY

Well, I was told I could have 3 chickens as my birthday gift last March and keep them at my partner's house, as he has a garden, and I had a yard. So, I got two and then two became four, then one went broody, so she was given some surrogate eggs, so our four quickly turned into ten! We rehomed three of the hens and a cockerel from the hatch, so now we have four hens and two cockerels!

After being told I was only allowed three, I have triumphantly now ended up with six. It would be more, but we don't have space for anymore.

I have had to since move into my partner's house look after them while he is at work.

When our broody hen was sitting on her eggs my son was so excited, he made a song up called Happy Hatch Day! He sang this song every day until the chicks hatched. From then on, he sat by our new mother hen and her babies and sang to them every day.

When the chicks were old enough for him to hold, he held them close to his face to feel the softness of their baby feathers. One of the said chicks took quite an interest in his eyes and pecked him straight in his eye! He never put another chick near his face again!

Natalie Mcteer – County Durham, Ireland

THE ORIGINAL FLUFFYBUTT LOVE

I was normal 3 chickens ago...

CHAPTER 31

HOW TO COUNT YOUR CHICKENS

So, for all you people who are told four chickens is enough or that you have too many, please redo your math's.

I have around thirty 2 legged things dwelling either in the house and the coop. Two of which are roosters. But I have zero chickens at the moment.

Why? This is why:

Are you sure you are counting your chickens correctly? Because there are specific rules to keep in mind while counting:

1. You do not count any eggs in the incubator because you do not count your chickens before they hatch.

2. You do not count chickens that were given as a gift be-

cause they were a present and are more properly considered a gift rather than a chicken.

3. You do not count any bird under 18 weeks old because they are too young to lay eggs, so they are considered juveniles rather than chickens.

4. You do not count bantams because bantams are considered bantams rather than chickens.

5. You do not count ornamental birds because they are ornamental and are considered yard art, folk art, or fine art rather than chickens.

6. You do not count birds beyond laying age because they are retired and do not lay eggs and are considered retirees rather than chickens.

7. You do not count birds in moult because they are in moult and missing feathers so cannot be properly considered as complete chickens.

8. You do not count males because they are protectors of the flock and are more accurately considered guard dogs rather than chickens.

9. You do not count laying hens because they produce eggs and thus are more accurately described as a food source rather than chickens.

10. You do not count sick or injured birds because they

are sick or injured and their disposition is in question, so they go on the injured or sick list, not on your list of chickens.

11. You do not count birds that are for sale or possibly for sale because they belong or will belong to someone else.

12. You do not count broody hens because you cannot even get close enough to count them.

13. You do not count freeloading chickens because they are not producing eggs, therefore they are not fully chicken.

Thus, if you follow the rules (and it is always good to follow the rules) you may only count healthy full-size female chickens that are not in moult and not a gift and are of laying age but not laying.

Happy counting!

Coupled with 'It's better to ask for forgiveness than it is permission' you can spend as much money as your heart desires!

Dawna June – Wisconsin, USA

CHAPTER 32

MENDIP CHICKENS

I grew up with my three brothers on a farm in the Mendip Hills of Somerset, that was an ancient old cloth mill and steeped in history. Friends likened it to the Darling Buds of May homestead.

We had plenty of room for our menagerie of birds and the incubator was often on, filled with rare breed pheasants, ducks and not to mention lots of chicken.

We have a river at the bottom of our garden, so wild mallard ducks would also gather at feeding time, among our dozens of chickens and guinea fowl (which my dad called Gleeneys!).

There was wild pheasant too. They would all, often reaching over hundred feathered friends, run at you the minute you walked outside the front door and gather expectantly at your feet. With clucking and squeaking sounds. You could imagine the excitement if you had the corn bucket in your hand as well!

They laid their eggs everywhere but the warm straw bedded nest box. We found dozens in the hay bales once.

We had one silky hen, who sat on ducks' eggs, hatched them and was treated as mum. She however did become quite confused and concerned when her 'babies' discovered the trout stream and decided to take the plunge. She would stand on the riverbank and cluck furiously at them!

All our birds lived harmoniously alongside each other. Our collie dog Roger, then Angus, never batted an eyelid at them. Which just proves we can live in harmony alongside each other.

We always had 'fun' at penning up time!

Our two cockerels at one time would try to outwait each other neither wanting to be the first into the coop! We often ended up chasing them around the coop, until they both went into bed!

Many years on now and they have a beautiful old cockerel George IX (or is it X...?) with his solitary lady hen. They are like an old married couple. He fusses over her and call her to any food and will not eat until she has finished. Such a true feathery gent. He follows my parents wherever they go. He will also come and sit next to them and nuzzle up to their legs.

Who needs a TV when you can sit and watch your hens? I cannot imagine not having grown up surrounded by such endearing animals and birds. They were part of our family and teach you to be caring and humble.

Sue Ball – Somerset, England

CHAPTER 33

CHICKEN CPR

Broody hen Merkel hatched one sweet little chick around teatime. All was well. But the next morning, there was no sign of it. Even though they were in their own separate brooder area, the baby had somehow got separated from mum in the night.

Eventually, I found its little body cold, stiff, and very dead. For reasons I still do not understand, I cupped it in my hands and breathed warm air on it from the depth of my lungs. After a while, I felt its stiff little body melt, and after about twenty minutes it showed signs of life. I do not have a brooder, so I put it back under mum, and hoped for the best. When I came back later, the little chick was loudly up and about – it had survived! We called her 'Little Princess'.

Apparently, this happens. It's one of the most amazing things that's ever happened to me.

THE ORIGINAL FLUFFYBUTT LOVE

If you find a cold, dead chick, please don't immediately give up on it. Stick it down your bra. Whatever it takes.

The saying is, it's not dead until it's warm and dead.

Shirley Acreman – Midlands, England

CHAPTER 34

DIVA DOINGS

Barbara Ann is a buff laced polish frizzle chicken. She is beautiful and very opinionated; some may say slightly scatter-brained.

The day she laid her first egg was a long, long day. It appeared she just could not decide where to lay and was very vocal about it, squawking loudly for hours. Of course, the nest boxes were not a good enough spot for her, she went in and out of the coop, protesting *all* day, finally settling on a spot behind the shed. After hours of sitting and placing bits of grass in just the right spot to make a comfy nest, she stood up, walked over to the fence and plopped out her egg there!

The endless hours of squawking, pacing and nest building, only the lay her egg out of the nest on the dirt! She is such a diva!

Mandy Watts – Queensland, Australia

N.B. As the author I can corroborate this story as my own Pretty (also a Poland Frizzle) has been known to badger me into letting her in and out of the back patio door approximately twenty-nine times in less than two hours while she decided whether she should lay in the dirty laundry basket in the house or somewhere else in the garden!

CHAPTER 35

ADDICTED VET

I started with six Brahmas, one, unfortunately, passed away so down to five - three of them being cockerels, then a stray chicken came into my work (I work at a veterinary practice) so I took him home to foster until a home was found - that failed miserably and he ended up getting in the boy gang with the other three cockerels. Seems like he might be a Braham cross too which was a nice surprise. I hoped for a while that he was a hen and have even called him Wanda the Wanderer. The name stuck but he is definitely a 'he'.

I planned to get three ex-batts and then the day before they were due *another* chicken came into work. A lady was walking her Labrador through the woods near a chicken farm.

He ran off and came back with a hen! We checked her over and then I got told I was taking her home since I am the crazy chicken lady!! I named her Queenie after Steve McQueen for her Great Escape. The ex-batts arrived the day after and made her part of their gang straight away.

In twelve years of working in Veterinary, I've never discovered a stray chicken. However, I'm sure at this rate more will come in and end up being added to my pack of chucks!!

Clare Hawkesby – Shropshire, England

If you are my neighbour, sooner or later you are going to see me chasing a chicken in my underwear!

CHAPTER 36

CARAVAN CHICKENS

My husband Dave said we could have three rescue chickens, so we prepared ourselves by buying a coop with six ft run attached.

When the day came to collect our girls, we ended up going all the way to Ashbourne in Derby, an hour down the road, to collect the rescues not registering that we could have collected them locally in Rotherham!

Anyways I was very concerned about the six chicks as it was icy, so I let them stay in the caravan instead of the coop. You can imagine the amount of work involved collecting poop, covering the seats with shower curtains and old duvet covers and washing them weekly.

We then bought another coop and a large cage and ended up getting another three, then another five. Then another coop and another four fancy breeds. We lost a few rescues, gained another nine and a hatched chick and two cocks, plus we received a late Christmas gift of four. So yes, we have loads. Along with our five cats and two dogs, a lot of work is required, and love given and received for one egg a day!

Judith Fletcher King – Sheffield, England

CHAPTER 37

CHICKEN CHUCKLES

Personally, I find it funny that all the neighbours on our lane are keeping an eye on our chickens as they decide to take themselves on walkies when I'm not home. I often get updates on how far they travelled and how various neighbours chased them back in for me. I now leave a sweeping brush by the back gate for neighbours to use if needed. The chooks, of course, are mortified by the sweeping brush!

Virginia Hill - Caernarfon, North Wales

* * * * *

All 10 of my birds took themselves for a walk over to my elderly neighbour's house (he is in his late 80s) he was working in his garage and they all started tapping him on the leg!! He told me he almost had a heart attack from the shock, which given his age makes me think he might not be exaggerating!

He walked them back to the garden and they all pootled along behind him as if they were model citizens. That was the day I found out my gate had broken!

Clare Hawkesby – Shropshire, England

* * * * *

Have you ever heard a chicken gag???

Miss Toffee was free ranging in the garden with her sisters, and our dog Ben was also enjoying the garden.

The girls were happily foraging when I heard something between a squawk and gagging. I turned round to see Miss Toffee frantically shaking her head and making this most horrendous noise. I ran over thinking she was choking on long grass or something but when I scooped her up..., well...I discovered she had got a mouth full of fresh dog poo and was actually gagging on it. She was not impressed! I, on the other hand, couldn't stop laughing!

I have always been a caring person and am well known by my elderly neighbours as someone they can call on day or night if they need anything. I started her caring at a young age of eight as both of my parents had complex health problems and I looked after them as best as I could. Later on in life I was involved in a road traffic accident and was badly injured, as a result, I developed fibromyalgia, PTSD and anxiety. Although I love looking after others, I do tend to forget about myself until I'm all fizzled out.

To help me relax more and de-stress, my husband finally caved in after ten years of nagging and allowed me to rescue some chickens. This was the best thing ever as it gives me a reason to step away from my busy household and have five minutes of peace with my fluffy family. Having chicken cuddles every day helps me to forget my troubles for five minutes. My children call me a crazy chicken momma as my love for chickens has spilt over into the living room where there are chicken ornaments galore!

Sarah Banner - Nottinghamshire, England

CHAPTER 38

BETTY

Betty came to live with me along with her friend Ethel, and together they had great adventures exploring my couple of acres of land. Every day they would find new exciting mischief to get into and things to explore. After a few months of happily exploring together, Ethel suddenly died with no warning.

Betty was devastated and fell into a complete slump, totally losing the will to live. I brought her indoors every day to keep her company and to make sure I could get food and water down her, as left to her own devices she would've starved herself to death she was so depressed.

Whilst this was going on, I was also trying to locate some more little chicken friends for her to cheer her up - in particular, Lavender Pekin bantams such as Betty is, but for the first time in years of keeping chickens, I couldn't find any for sale anywhere. And so, Betty and I ambled along together, and she gradually stopped being so sad and started taking an interest in the things I was doing as I was going about my day. For example, if I cut my grass on my ride-on mower, rather than being scared of it, Betty would hop on too and enjoy the ride around the garden. Anything I did, and anywhere I went, Betty followed along.

Then one day, a miracle of miracles, I managed to track down two Lavender Pekin bantam girls, but it was a six-hour round trip to get them. I looked at Betty's little face and thought, 'Well, it's got to be done.' So off I set to get these two lovely Lavender girls. Well, Betty *hated* them on sight and wouldn't have anything to do with them. All she wanted was me, and she got worse and worse for wanting my attention. If I put her outside with the other girls she would cry and sob, throwing herself at every door and window until I let her in. I never knew a chicken could cry and have a tantrum till I met Betty! So gradually she got her way and spent more and more time with me, until I gave in, bought her a cat bed to sleep in and let her live indoors permanently.

To my surprise, it took about a week to have her 100% toilet trained, and about Twenty-four hours for her to get addicted to TV! Now that manipulative little chicken has found her way to sleeping in her little cat bed on my passenger pillow at night. It's very sweet when she wakes up in the night and clambers out of her bed to cuddle up with me for a few minutes before climbing back into her own bed for the rest of the night. She's a bit too used to my routine now though, come 8 PM she sits on my chest and stares at me, chuntering in chicken speak, "Isn't it past our bedtime? I want to go get settled upstairs in bed."

Nowadays I have a lot more chickens who she quite likes, and although she'll wander out to play with them, a couple of hours later, she's knocking at the door and throwing a tantrum to come back in for a cuddle and a treat. She's decided I'm her companion now and we're just little housemates that take care of each other, I feel her love and gratitude in every little chicken cuddle I feel in the middle of the night before she gets back in her own bed. But make no mistake, she rules the roost!

K.L. Smith – East Yorkshire, England

CHAPTER 39

MIRACLE

I used to volunteer for the British Hen Welfare Trust, which rescue spent hens from battery cages and re-home them to people who keep them as pets in their gardens. Depending on the farm, some rescues can be heart-breaking as the hens can come out with broken legs/wings, bald through being pecked so much through boredom by other hens, terrified, starving and traumatized!

One weekend in July, whilst taking the hens out of the crates, a volunteer placed a 'dead' chicken in a bucket presuming it dead as there were no signs of life. About half an hour later I looked in the bucket and put my hand on her cold little skinny body and to my amazement could see a tiny pulse in her bald thigh!

I picked her up, wrapped her in a towel and held her against my body to try to warm her up. I made her a hot water bottle and kept rotating it around her body. I knew it was a long shot that she'd survive but no one was going to stop me from giving her that chance.

After a while, I could feel an awfully slow irregular heartbeat and could feel little twitches going on. I stood in the sun and huffed on her comb to try to warm her up. After about an hour there were more and more little head and feet movements. I was convinced she was alive, and it was not just nerves twitching.

Eventually, she was standing on her own, so I gave her a small amount of food and water. I called her Miracle and bought her home with me with a little friend I called Mermaid as she fell in the water. Miracle made a perfect pet hen. When I came into the garden, she would run so fast towards me, let me pick her up and make little chirping noises to me. I used to think she was saying 'thank you' for saving her life.

In the end, she only lived one year and 5 days as she developed crop problems and struggled to eat. I tried everything, including liquidizing her food, but it didn't help, and it was kinder to have her put to sleep, but she had a lovely second chance at life with me and her other hen friends.

Miracles story made me realize these hens can look dead but all they need is time to recover.

Tiggy Fuller – Surrey, England

CHAPTER 40

BOMBER

We were lucky enough to have a lovely cottage with a huge garden in Herefordshire - where we were spending a bit of time. The garden was about half an acre but all it had in it was an empty veg plot, 2 apple trees and a Peony bush. So, when a neighbour offered us some rescue hens, we thought they'd fill up a corner. A hen house was built, wire enclosure put up and the ladies arrived. They were a manky looking bunch, thrown out of a broiler shed as being unlikely to live very long.

They had half-formed wings, twisted legs, missing and misshaped feet and they were barely more than chicks, but they gobbled up everything they were given and grew. One really grew and it dawned on us we had a cockerel. He was big, white, and fiercely protective of his ladies and he got named 'Bomber' after a big, blonde-haired military mate of my husbands.

Me, he would tolerate - if I came bearing food but he

loved my old man and spent hours poking around the gravel as himself tinkered at his motorbike. The drawback was that he went for anyone who came up the drive, at a height of 4 feet, huge wings flapping and vicious spurs at the ready. He was made to stay in the back garden when we had visitors. But that had its drawbacks especially when we had our mates round for beers and a BBQ.

One night rather too many beers had been drunk and the lads, one in particular, Roger, was feeling no pain. Bomber and the ladies were shut in their big run, but that wasn't going to stop Roger. "Can I go and stroke your chickens?" he asked my husband. "Well...you can try," the husband told him, "But watch the cockerel - he's a bit protective".

Roger scoffs "It's just a chicken!" and saunters off. He got into the run OK and then Bomber decided enough was enough, took off, squawking and flapping and fastened himself by his spurs round Roger's thigh. He knocked him over and then began attacking Roger's family jewels. The yells were heard ¼ of a mile away, for several minutes while we all laughed and let Bomber have his fun.

Eventually, once it was obvious Roger was actually bleeding, my husband went and removed Bomber, picking him up and petting him like a large cat. Roger was taken off so first aid and whiskey could be administered. Roger's party trick became pulling down his trousers to show the scars on his thighs, but he never asked to "stroke the chickens" again!

Bomber's other claim to fame wasn't quite as dramatic. My husband went out to round him and the girls up and put them in for the night one autumn evening but came running back moments later saying Bomber was down, looked ill and couldn't walk.

We got a cardboard box, put him in it with some straw and water and popped him in the shed, fully expecting to have a dead bird the next morning. Far from it. Bomber woke us up with loud crowing at about 6 am. He was right as rain. We took him up the garden - expecting him to go up to his girls but no, he legged it across the garden, to the apple tree, which had loads of windfall apples under it. We followed him and realized why he had been falling over the night before. The windfalls were fermenting, and he'd got drunk eating them!

Bess Elle – Herefordshire, England

JESSIE SHEDDEN

I'm not great at math...

...but adding chickens and subtracting drama solves most of my problems.

CHAPTER 41

CHICKENS RULE THE ROOST

In May we went for three, a maximum of four hens. However, we came back home with forty-eight chicks! Twenty-six turned out to be roosters, so that left us with twenty-two hens and chose to keep 3 roosters. In September two hens went broody and decided that we needed some more! Ok! So, on 1st October we had another fourteen chickens.

Then in December, another hen went broody! Ok, sweet mommy, you deserve to have babies too! So, another five hatched just before Christmas. Just after New Year's Day, one rebellious hen start broody too! So now we have another 8 on the way! OMG! It's not me! They always decide how many chickens we need!

Lena Zaiceva– Worcestershire, England

CHAPTER 42

CAESAR

For a long while, I've rescued and rehomed ex-commercial hens, with Fresh Start for Hens. Most of my flock of hens have quirks, foibles and special needs. I specialize in keeping the 'unfit for rehoming' ladies and nursing them back to health and giving them a permanent home. This one's a special needs rescue with a difference....a huge Shamo/Asil type cockerel now called Caesar.

Our previous resident rooster, Sylvester (also special needs, he had a hatch defect which meant he had one leg several inches than the other) had recently died, at the grand old age of eight, so there was space in our lives for another cockerel, but it had to be the right one.

Caesar was spotted, presumably dumped, by a member of the public. They notified one of my fellow Fresh Start for Hens volunteers who was able to go and retrieve him. After much chasing around a stable yard and wrangling with the strength of a large cockerel who was frightened and really didn't want to be caught, he was safely captured. Once picked up, the sight and smell of his injury was evident and stomach-churning. He had a missing eye and a huge plug of solidified infection had stretched and filled the socket. As a Shamo/Asil breed, this may well have been the resulting of being used for fighting.

He was taken into the temporary care of another Fresh Start volunteer for assessment and to begin treatment and then travelled 100 miles up country in a van full of rescue hens on one of our rehoming days to take up residence and complete his treatment with us.

He had surgery to remove the plug of infection, the socket was packed, and this was removed and replaced twice a week alongside antibiotics and pain relief. He lived in a dog crate, safe from the risk of further infection, during this process and we had regular cuddles to socialize him and garner his trust. He responded well; he'd settle down on my lap or sprawled across my chest for snoozes and would give me what I came to call 'long neck loves' stretching his neck out and holding his head against mine.

After a couple of weeks, we were confident he was infection-free and his eye socket was left to slowly heal closed, which it did perfectly. Now for the fun of introductions! I hadn't anticipated how *big* this boy would be once he'd recovered and gained weight...he was almost 5kg now he was back to full health.

We initially gave him some time in the garden on his

own; he was very interested in the hens, as they were in him. He made straight for their walk-in run, where he paced up and down, talking away to them from the outside and they did likewise from the inside.

So far, so good. Supervised free-range time seemed like the next stage so out the girls came. This didn't go as planned. Poor Caesar was terrified and ran screaming to hide behind my legs, as far as such a big fella can hide behind them that is! I'd underestimated how psychologically damaged this poor soul was and my suspicion that he'd been used in fighting seemed to be correct. I can't think of any other reason for him to be so frightened of a flock of ten lopsided, middle-aged hens.

So, the next stage of introductions consisted of him having a daily sit in my lap on a garden chair while the hens pecked around us. He came to relax and accept that they weren't going to hurt him after a few days of doing this.

Within a week, he was happily sharing scatter treats with them at a safe distance and within a fortnight he'd decided he quite liked them and was living alongside them in the coop and run. He's been here for around 4 months now and is a much-loved addition to our flock.

The girls mostly adore him too, although I think they'll be happy when his testosterone levels settle down a bit! He's so tall that they can't reach to preen him, but he's discovered how to manage this little problem. He does the most heart-warming thing. When he wants to be preened, the hens get a bit of his "long neck love" too, he reaches down and gently head bumps them to signal that he wants a fuss, a bit likes cats do to their humans. The hens will happily oblige for as long as he keeps himself within their reach. Shared dust baths are comical; he has no concept of how much of a space hogger he is or how much he kicks the girls while kicking the dirt about, I can all but see the eye rolls they give him as they give up and move away.

It's an absolute joy to see him happy, healthy, confident and behaving just the way he should be doing.

We still miss Sylvester but offering a home to Caesar and helping to heal his physical and psychological hurt has been a fitting way to fill the gap.

Emma Mitchell – Leicestershire, England

CHAPTER 43

WHOMIN THE HUMAN CHICKEN

Whomin the human chicken was an egg that hatched as an only survivor. The breeder had no other indoor chickens and being winter, they didn't want to put her with the flock, so they gave her to us. It was decided that she should have a home that could nurture her and teach her to eventually be a chicken while being allowed to be safely in the house until she was ready, as she had been hand-raised by humans since she peeped and loved her human family.

My daughter, Lily decided on the name 'Whomin' because this little chick thought she was a human. She slept in Lily's bed with her each night and roamed her room like an adventurous toddler. Everywhere Lily went, Whomin went too. Anything Lily ate, Whomin ate too. Lily being a vegetarian started asking for McDonald's cheeseburgers with extra extra pickles and I finally questioned her, only to find out Whomin's favourite snack food was McDonald's pickles!

Lily loved waking up most mornings with Whomin next to her, or on her and she would often be woken up by her pecking her in the mouth.

Come spring once it warmed up, we did eventually bring her outside with the flock to teach her to be a chicken. But to this day, she still comes running for her pickles or daddy's coffee! She also jumps in my car to go for car rides! She does have a boyfriend now who she sticks by for the most part, but she loves her humans still the same! If we are outside, she always comes running up to us, jumps on our shoulders and lets us know that we will always be her human family. She taught us the importance of bonding, and how strong that trust can be between a chicken and a human and how healing they can be to one's soul.

Dawna June – Wisconsin, USA

CHAPTER 44

A KITCHEN FULL OF CHICKENS

I started with three peacocks, good intentions and no clue. It wasn't long before I went on to add ten chickens. Soon you realize you are now in love, and it's time to add ducks. Fast forward I wake up from being in a coma and find I've been had and all my ducks are drakes! In that case, I must add more ducks. The husband says "No more!!" Of course, I ignore him and start sneaking chickens home wondering if he will notice because it's funny! I buy an incubator, then I buy two. After all, it's his fault after he tricked me into thinking one of my peacocks was a hen.

I hatch chicken chicks to keep potential peafowl chicks' company but sadly the peafowl chicks are too young. Then you realize you can't sell chicks because you *looooove* them too much and after all no one loves chickens like you do! The husband says, "No more." You ignore that fool.

Finally, the peafowl starts giving you fertile eggs, so now

it's all systems go! You discover you looooove hatching and start hatching for others. Your kitchen is full of chicks from April to October. Husband begs "No more." You laugh maniacally, and carry on anyway realizing you may, just may have a chicken math problem!

You learn people don't want cockerels so spend months each year telling people "Just because you can, it doesn't mean you should hatch chicks unless you are prepared to deal with all the cockerels." Karma takes her sweet revenge, and you manage to hatch *all* cockerels in your last hatch of the year. Luckily for you, you can keep cockerels, but you still haven't managed to hatch one peacock, just peahens so the hatching will continue. Wonderful husband has given up saying no more and is now building new pens.... And that is chicken math's in Welsh!

Wolfie – Yellow Moutain, Wales

MEET THE CONTRIBUTORS

Joe Nutkins

Joe Nutkins lives in Essex, England with husband Jon, twelve rescue hens, two rescue cockerels, five heritage hens, six rescue ducks, six heritage ducks, three quail, a house duck and two Norwich Terriers! She is Kennel Club Accredited Dog Trainer and Certified Trick Dog Trainer and has previously auditioned her dogs on Britain's Got Talent and owns the world's first trick duck – Echo. For videos of Echo and the gang look up Echo Trick Ducks Excellent Adventures on FB, Dog Training for Essex and Suffolk on FB or CassnTay on Twitter or Instagram!

Wolfie

Wolfie had a fabulous life, busy career, rode motorbikes and spent weekends dancing in fields with her friends. After waking from a long coma and mystery illness her life had completely changed. She had to learn to think, talk, walk, use her hands again. The trauma suffered in ITU left her deeply traumatized. With no physio or rehab available Wolfie had a choice. Give up or try every day to keep ongoing. Despite the pain, Wolfie walks every day. If it wasn't for her chickens, ducks and peacocks she would have given up. The birds have been her inspiration, her physio, her friends, her reason to live and to keep on putting one foot in front of the other. You can keep up with

Wolfie and her birds at Yellow Mountain Peacocks on Facebook.

Mel Lazenby

Mel has owned hens from childhood and has been involved in hen rescues since 2007, specializing in disabled and sick hens, especially leg injuries. She was a coordinator for Little Hen Rescues Cambridge collection for many years before it had sadly to close. She now volunteers for the BHWT (British Hen Welfare Trust) here in the UK, rescuing ex caged hens, being part of the farm collection team, and also provides rehabilitation when required. A strict vegan, and has been since 2012, after having been vegetarian since the age of seventeen. She trained as an embalmer and worked in a human dissecting room for Cambridge university for ten years. Then moved to the vet school for a further ten years. Due to ill health, she is now medically retired, so spends all her time faffing about with her animals, in what is affectionately known as the 'petting zoo' down her garden. She lives with her partner Darran, three cats, guinea pigs, quail and hens.

Eden Zook

Eden Zook lives on a small farm in Deerfield, New Hampshire (USA) with her husband Bryan and their twenty-one animal family members; including cat, chickens, parrots, dogs, horses, and mini horses. She is the founder/trainer/behaviour consultant of Canine Karma LLC; a dog behaviour and training organization. She also spent 16 years in the animal shelter field before opening Canine Karma in 2015. She is always on the quest to strengthen the human-animal bond and is currently pursuing a second business offering soul level animal communication and reiki services. You can reach out to Eden via email at caninekarmatrainer@gmail.com

Margaret Hope

Mags suffered many years of agoraphobia anxiety and depression. After "accidentally" rescuing three hens she had no choice but to start going outside. Slowly she recovered and has since rescued many more girls from slaughter. She truly believes they rescued her and not her them.

Sarah Seleta Nothnagel

Sarah, thirty-seven, lives in Wellington, Colorado, USA with her husband Michael, daughter Joy, two cats, three Old-Fashioned German Shepherds, and ten chickens. She worked for ten years as a Certified Veterinary Technician, before returning to school to become a Medical Laboratory Scientist. She currently works in the Colorado State University Veterinary Teaching Hospital's Clinical Pathology Department where she can utilize her knowledge of veterinary medicine and medical laboratory science concurrently. Her friends would describe her as outgoing, personable, compassionate, quick-witted, and funny. Though her favourite topic of conversation and hobby is chickens, she also enjoys spending time in stunning the Colorado outdoors by running, camping, and Jeeping.

Aspen Palmer

Aspen Palmer is a musician and hobbyist artist living in the south-east of England. Shortly after being hospitalized for their mental health, Aspen's family rescued three ex-battery hens, and a love of chickens was born. Watching these hens recover and thrive from their trauma gave Aspen the courage to recover from their own. Several years later, the flock consists of twelve hens and two roosters, and Aspen proudly volunteers for the British Hen Welfare Trust.

Nicky Dawson

Nicky Dawson has lived in Hampshire, and Essex before settling in Norfolk in 2001. She has worked as a London magazine journalist and editor, a graphic designer - with a claim to fame designing the signs for toilets at the Duke and Duchess of York's wedding - a secondary school and FE teacher and a senior leader for Children's Social Care managing national programs and winning several awards. But she gave all that up to become a therapeutic foster carer.

Lizzie Harling

Lizzie is the author of The Good Life Crewe blog telling the many varied and ridiculous escapades of allotment life in the UK. The allotment adventures are not solely restricted to chickens but the many eccentricities of daily life as a plot holder including rescuing jackdaws, building ponds and keeping bees! She also runs Poultry Paraplegics, a tiny business creating customized wheelchairs for disabled poultry. Her allotment is home to a flock of chickens of all different breeds and a rather useless but friendly cockerel. You can find her blog at www.thegoodlifecrewe.com and Poultry Paraplegics on Facebook and Instagram.

Wendy Steele

Wendy says she is not a normal person as she was a nurse for about three centuries but then, one day, for a bet, she did a law degree, whilst working full time as a nurse and ended up being a lawyer. The girl that had the bet only lasted three months doing her degree! She lives on the beautiful Isle of Anglesey where she has a holiday let attached to her home, and there are many weeks that her guests go down the garden to see her girlies (who are all named after Wendy's dead aunties) and stand there with their bottoms in the air talking for ages to the girlies! They don't have a clue that Wendy can see that they all have full-blown conversations with her chickens!

Dawna June

Dawna June is a recent stay at home Mom and wife of eight kids and a grandmother to one. She has a small hobby farm with chickens, ducks, geese, guineas and potbelly pigs. A few cats as well as a puppy! Her quote as she takes care of the family, rescuing unwanted birds and raising the kiddos is "bring on the chaos". She recently has embarked on a journey in finding out the youngest kid is moderate to severe on the Autism Spectrum and is hoping that one day the chickens will be just as therapeutic for him as they are for her!

Dean Burton

Dean Burton and his wife Gemma both served in the army – Dean for twelve years with three tours of Iraq and one in Afghanistan and Gemma completing three tours of Iraq so their lives have been adventurous, to say the least. They had 2 children whilst in the army and chose to settle in Abergavenny, South Wales. When they moved to a little bungalow with just over a third of an acre, they decided to have a few chickens which in chicken math's means one +two = seventy-six. Dean suffers from PTSD from Afghanistan and soon learnt that spending time with these beautiful birds really helped with his stress levels and he becomes calm again. Gemma claims not to be bothered about them, but every Saturday finds herself covered in bird poop as she cleans out all the coops.

E.V. Dawson

E.V. Dawson is an author, homesteader, service dog handler, wife and mother. She has two dogs, two cats, seven hens, and a rooster. She enjoys knitting, gardening, and baking in her spare time.

Wendy Rurak

Wendy Rurak is a modern-day St Francis. She has an uncanny knack with animals seeming to understand their language. They flock to her (pun intended) and she currently raises ducks, chickens, and turkeys as well as maintaining a seven-member dog pack and we must not forget the two cats! At one point, she even rescued two arctic foxes from an animal auction, who are now living in a sanctuary since they would not survive in the wild on their own. There are many lovely facets to Wendy's life including her being a mother and grandmother. Her family live in Portland Oregon, but Wendy found her own sanctuary in sweet home Alabama. Although she misses her roots, Alabama offers her the room for her endeavours. She's a full-time government worker and a student pursuing a master's degree and ultimately a PhD which will free her up to be able to incorporate her psychology counselling degree with her love of animals. She has a great sense of humour and reminds us all that there's no sense in being broody! She can be reached at PO box 54 Vinemont, Alabama 35179 or by email at wendystdys@yahoo.com.

Marion Petersen

Marion Petersen is a small hobby farmer in Southern California, specializing in Serama chickens. Growing up on a working ranch, Marion learned a lot about animal husbandry. Marion is also a reiki master, psychic and medium working directly out of her farm.

Virginia Hill

Virginia grew up on a smallholding and has loved animals all her life. Being able to keep chickens brings back nice childhood memories. Animals helped Virginia to get out the bed every day even during depressive episodes. She studied biology at University intending to become an ecologist but somehow ended up working as a bridge engineer. If she won the lottery, she'd buy a smallholding, lots more poultry and a black horse.

Connie Sides

Connie is a mom of five sons, two of whom have autism, and two of whom are adopted. The only girls she has are her two Dobermans names Stella and Ziti. She and her husband decided to leave the city once their sons had graduated so they could focus on country living and expand their dog training business. Since moving they designed and built a coop to hold twenty+ chickens, just in case they decided they wanted more than just six or seven. However, they are now bumping the threshold of a hundred and are several coops into their hobby.

Linda Eblett

Linda Eblett moved from England to Scotland in 2014 after her hubby was constantly up there on his motorbike and she jokingly said, 'we should all just go live there'! The first thing she did was buy some ex-batt hens and that was it, she was hooked! She started breeding Poland bantams and shipping their eggs to Finland and Greece. Her beautiful, baldy husband hates her hobby, her garden has been wrecked by her little feathered pals, but she promises to fix that when she no longer has them, whenever that may be!

Bonney A R

Bonney grew up in a small country town and now lives in Brisbane with her partner and animal family. Growing up she had a rough childhood, and always turned to the animals she loved, especially her chickens. She has since started rescuing animals including birds and chickens.

Stephanie F. Kelley

Stephanie F. Kelley grew up on a farm in Alabama, USA. She has always loved animals and her dream as a young girl was to become a vet. Instead of becoming a veterinarian, she became a healthcare worker for many years. She has two grown kids and three grandbabies and has trekked around forty four of the fifty states of America driving a big rig for a few months She now only works at home tending to the farm and her beloved flock of chickens and ducks as well as their two dogs and cats. She spends her spare time painting, wood carving, restoring furniture, building things from scrap wood, and machine embroidery.

Amanda Quire

Amanda grew up in a city in Kentucky having never been around chickens. When COVID-19 started, and she couldn't find eggs and her 'survivalist' husband decided they needed to be able to support themselves. So, on Mother's Day, she got chickens! She is a mother of four, a foster parent and a paramedic. Recently she and her husband have become youth pastors. No matter who comes to the house, they always love seeing the flock!

Rebecca Robinson

Rebecca first became a chicken mum aged eleven when a little brown hen ran out of the bushes the day her parents moved into a new house. Turns out the previous owners left her, didn't want her back and it was the start of her love for fluffy butts! Now a married mum to three girls who also have the same love of chucks, she juggles full-time work, renovating an old farmhouse, playing the guitar and is the lead singer in a rock band. Along with the chickens, she has a dog, two rats, a snake and two Giant African Land snails and claims to be powered by her love of Jack Daniels!

Clare Hinkley

Clare Hinkley first came to be a chicken owner by chance when they were left behind as pets. Being a person who does not know how to sit still and relax, she decided that working full time in her local council, part-time as a lifeguard, and part-time as a police officer, as well as being a netball lover she had a few minutes spare to increase the small number of three hens by one. Then another, followed by a rescue here and there, taking in lonely hens needing a home, plus two unexpected cockerels. Currently, she has ten chickens with plans for more. Why not? she asks they are the best thing about any garden!

Emily Rose Thorp

Emily lives with her partner, three-year-old son, and a menagerie of pets including six hens and three cockerels. When she left school, she decided to work with animals as an educational and therapeutic tool for children and young adults with disabilities and has volunteered and worked for several charities doing this. When not cleaning out the menagerie, Emily enjoys photography, walking and gardening, well, what's left of it anyway!

Jolene Kunde

Jolene is a Spiritual Healer, HMUA and a professional Boudoir and Fantasy Photographer. She is the owner of The Upper Peninsula of Michigan's Premier Boudoir studio, UPLifted Boudoir Photography. www.upliftedboudoir.com Jolene is an avid animal lover who grew up on a farm and has always had a way with animals. She currently has an Irish wolfhound mix, two dachshund puppies, three cats and nineteen chickens. In her spare time, she can be found hiking in nature with her camera, three dogs, her three cats (that *refuse* to be excluded), and spending time sitting in her yard meditating or reading a good book with a chicken or two (three, four, or five...) on her lap.

James Weatherup

James Weatherup is twenty-four years old from the Emerald Isle of Northern Ireland situated outside the hills of country Antrim where he lives with his mum, dad, brother, and sister. James is country through and through, by day he works on his father's pedigree dairy, beef, and sheep farm. He is often found during summer showing his pedigree Holsteins and purebred poultry at shows, he is also a judge of dairy cattle and poultry too. James is most well-known for his stud of Poland's and has won many awards at the highest level through the UK and most recently won the 2020 Exhibitor of the Year award. He has sent his Poland breeding lines as far as the Isle of Bermuda and Singapore. James is the official Poland Clubs Northern Ireland Representative. He is a fun honest guy and loves having good laugh on a night out with friends in his free time. World of Polands on Facebook and Instagram pages has taken off over the last few years and James enjoys talking to people all over the world through this and discussing the finer points of the breed.

Emma Mitchell

Emma grew up in inner-city Nottingham where she trained as a mental health nurse, qualifying in 1989. She continues to work in this field and holds the role of clinical nurse specialist/ safeguarding lead within a very busy service. She moved to rural Leicestershire when her son left home for university, where she could upsize her hen pen and live a more sustainable lifestyle. In her spare time, she volunteers for Fresh Start for Hens and hosts a collection point for them regularly. She currently has ten rescue hens (most with special needs) and a rescued one-eyed cockerel. When partner Sean moved in with her, he also became actively involved with hen rescue as well as bringing his rescue cat and dog into the family.

Libby Downes

Libby is a Backyard Chicken Fancier, Gardener, Cook, Traveler, Restorer, Renovator, Knowledge Seeker and Phlebotomist. Due to COVID-19 Libby is currently performing specimen/swab collections at a COVID-19 testing drive-thru. As a "fun project" in 2020, she decided to transform a cubby house into a coop. The result is a cute little suburban chook house that sits under the shade of a mango tree for the hot Australian sun. Libby's girls are Silkies and are named Audrey, Selina and Laverne.

Marissa Troxclair

Marissa Troxclair is a novice homesteader and Serama breeder who lives a quiet life in the beautiful Pacific Northwest with a husband, several cats, two goats, and an unknown number of chickens and quail. Her other pastimes include obsessively delving into the culinary arts, gardening, reading, sewing, and building things with reclaimed wood.

Natalie McTeer

Natalie Mcteer is a mum of five, a partner, and a crazy chicken lady who works from home in direct sales. She lives in the northeast of England and currently has five chickens, two dogs, four cats, a rabbit and a guinea pig, all as support animals.

Sue Ball

Sue has two daughters, who love to visit the family farm she grew up on where her family have kept chicken for over a hundred years, dating back to her grandparents with many a tale to tell. She currently works in supporting autistic adults and now has her own menagerie of four-legged, two-legged and finned friends!

Shirley Acreman

Shirley has been a small-scale keeper of pet chickens for twenty-five+ years. When she retired, her goals were to breed Buff Sussex and learn German.

Mandy Watts

Mandy Watts is an Australian in her fifty's, living in Toowoomba, Queensland. She is a keen home gardener, a crazy chicken lady. Her part-time job is crocheting hats for chickens, selling them on Etsy. She runs an Instagram account called @herechookchook where she shares her heartfelt chicken stories, garden pics and brings many a smile to the faces of her followers.

Clare Hawkesby

Clare lived in Bristol for thirty years before moving to the countryside county of Shropshire. Finally having a huge country garden meant being able to get two or three chickens to start living "The Good Life". Ten chickens later and she is still accepting new waifs and strays from her job at a veterinary hospital. Who knew that stray chickens were actually a thing?!

Judith Fletcher King

Jude works as a Prevention Officer for Sheffield City Council, having worked previously in learning disabilities, and also for the Department of Work and Benefits. She learnt to ride a motorcycle after being passionate about them for years and now owns quite a collection. She is a member of Sheffield's Independent Bikers and Rotherham's Lions Pride Bikers. Jude and her husband David own two lovely caravans in a Scottish Holiday Park. When not in Rotherham with their two dogs, five cats, twenty-six hens and two cockerels, she loves to spend time watercolour painting, drawing, kayaking, fishing and getting to one with nature.

Sarah Banner

Sarah Banner is based in Nottingham, England. At the age of sixteen, Sarah joined St John's Ambulance Brigade and enjoyed taking part in first aid duties, first aid competition's and going on holidays as a carer. Now she is a full-time mum of four children who are her world. As well as homeschooling her children and Sarah is also a full-time carer for her husband who has a brain injury.

K.L. Smith

K. L. Smith is a writer of both comedy and thrillers – plus the occasional ghost story when persuaded. When she's not writing she can usually be found driving everyone around her to distraction with her many hobbies and projects. She's worked with birds of prey all of her life but now spends her days playing with chickens - much to her falcons' annoyance. Her has currently ten books in the humour, thrillers and supernatural field. She can be contacted at ww.klsmithbooks.com

Tiggy Fuller

Tiggy Fuller is fifty-five years old and a *huge* animal lover. She has kept pet chickens in her back garden for fifteen years. She is also a hairdresser but regrets not being an RSPCA inspector when she left school. She knows she'd have been great at the job as she cares very deeply for the welfare of animals, does not believe in locking any animal in a cage and just gets great pleasure in seeing them being allowed to live their lives exactly as nature intended. She volunteers for a chicken rescue charity and has seen firsthand the bad state these hens come out of the battery cages in and has had to pick up the pieces as best she could from the cruelty of man.

Bess Elle

Bronk and Bess are both regular soldiers, who have spent most of their careers fighting in someone else's back yard. However, they always had a bolt- hole at home, which was their cottage in rural Herefordshire, and when they had a rare couple of years with no long postings, they decided to have some rescue hens and a cockerel. The cockerel took his position in a military household very seriously as you can read in this book!

Lena Zaiceva

Lena Zaiceva is mum of two boys and two girls and was born in the LSSR part of USSR, which is now known as Lithuania. Originally her roots are from Siberia in Russia, where she spent all her life living in towns and animals like cows, horses and chickens existed only in the pages of a book. She moved to the UK in 2012 and in May 2020 she unexpectedly turned into a chicken mummy. Now her flock contains over forty hens and cockerels, but she will likely get more as she's already started thinking about moving to a rural area where she can experience even more happiness (aka chickens), as she is well and truly addicted!

SHARE WITH US

I would love to hear your reactions to the stories in this book. Please let me know what your favourite stories were and how they affected you.

I also invite you to send us stories you would like to see published in future editions of Fluffybutt Love. You can either send me your own story or stories written by others that you have enjoyed.

Send submission to hey@jessieshedden.com or find me on Facebook under Jessie Shedden and send me a private message.

You can also visit our Facebook Group: facebook.com/groups/loveoffluffybutts

I hope you enjoy reading this book as much as I have enjoyed compiling, editing and writing it.

WHO IS JESSIE SHEDDEN?

In the past I would have shuffled my feet, looked at the floor and mumbled my name, but not today. Today I will look you right in the eye and grinning say "I'm a chicken-loving, cult-escaping badass!"

You, of course, will look at me with equal part puzzlement and part awe.

Openly acknowledging to the world at a large that I am a certified crazy-chicken lady is a splash of the bold (thanks Trivento!), but cult-escaping *too*?!

As I document in my memoir Tomorrow's Not Promised (available an amzn.to/3kueDJQ) I spent the first thirty years of my life growing up in a strict religious cult, and the last three making up for lost time.

When I am not helping others escape the cult I was in, you will find me in my office with at least one of my chooks gathering stories from all around the globe for the Fluffybutt Love book series.

Pre COVID19 days I enjoyed travelling with my trusty camera by my side, nowadays I spend the time reading or being guest interviewed on all manner of podcasts. I have been featured in The Sun Newspaper, on BBC Radio, Somerset Life and in a range of other books.

I'm also an internationally published model, have hosted modelling events, trained in catwalk routines, and written for Medium, Elephant Journal and ThriveGlobal. Back in the days of shows, I was a Classic American Car photographer and as a hobby, I breed and keep rare breed bantam chickens. And lastly, I am a massive 1950's pinup, Dolly Parton, Country and Western lover.

You can find me at

Facebook: facebook.com/jessiejshedden and Fluffybutt Love: facebook.com/fluffybuttloves

Instagram: instagram.com/jessieshedden/

Twitter: twitter.com/JessieShedden

Website: jessieshedden.com

MORE FLUFFYBUTT LOVE?

We are always looking for more stories to include in future editions of Fluffybutt Love. Stories must be at least 500 words and uplift or inspire. Either pop over to our Facebook Group or send me a personal message.

Page: https://www.facebook.com/fluffybuttloves/

Group: https://www.facebook.com/groups/loveoffluffybutts/

Profile: https://www.facebook.com/jessiejshedden/

You may submit an original piece or something you clip out of the local newspaper/magazine or hear from a friend. It may be something you've had on your fridge door or experienced personally and has left an impression.

In addition to future series of Fluffybutt Love, some other books we have planned are Fluffybutt Love for Ducks, Fluffybutt Love for Peacocks, Fluffybutt Love for Parrots.

All you need to send is three things:

1) Your story of at least 500 words (remember to provide context and set the scene, Where are you? Who is involved? Etc.)
2) What name and place should be credited at the end of the story? *E.G. Jane Smith, Massachusetts, USA*
3) A short one-paragraph third-person bio. (See the contributor's section for inspiration.)

MORE IN THE BOOK SERIES

I am already working on books 2 and 3 in the series which includes a Special Rescue Edition!

Want to be sure you never miss hearing about future books?

Pop over my newsletter which is managed entirely by my gorgeous girls!

Join Chicken Chatter Newsletter: https://pages.jessieshedden.com/chicken-chatter/

Special Rescue Edition of the Fluffybutt Love series!

GLOSSARY

BHWT: British Hen Welfare Trust – an organization dedicated to saving and rehoming commercial laying hens throughout the United Kingdom.

FSFH: Fresh Start for Hens - a not for profit organization, run entirely by volunteers who are dedicated to rehoming hens from the commercial egg production sector.

Occluder: an implement that is used to cover or stop up a hole in the heart.

Rat-arsed: British slang. : very drunk.

Rooster/Roo: a male domestic fowl; a cock.

RSPCA: The Royal Society for the Prevention of Cruelty to Animals is a charity operating in England and Wales that promotes animal welfare.

Printed in Great Britain
by Amazon